USE THE
GOOD
DISHES™

FINDING JOY IN EVERYDAY LIFE

DR. ELAINE DEMBE

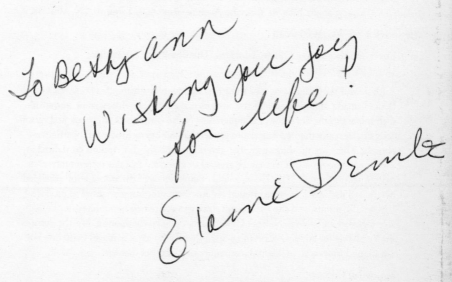

*To Betty ann
Wishing you joy
for life!*

Elaine Dembe

MACMILLAN CANADA
TORONTO

First published in Canada in 2000 by
Macmillan Canada, an imprint of CDG Books Canada

Copyright © Elaine Dembe 2000

Canadian Cataloguing in Publication Data

Dembe, Elaine, 1948-
  Use the good dishes : finding joy in everyday life

Includes index.
ISBN 0-7715-7677-3

1. Middle aged persons – Conduct of life. 2. Self-actualization (Psychology) in middle age. I. Title.
BJ169.D45 2000   158.1'084'4   C00-931063-0

This book is available at special discounts for bulk purchases by your group or organization for sales promotions, premiums, fundraising, and seminars. For details, contact: CDG Books Canada Inc., 99 Yorkville Avenue, Suite 400, Toronto, ON, M5R 3K5.

   3 4 5 6 WC 04 03 02 01

Cover and text design: Gillian Tsintziras, The Brookview Group Inc.
Cover Photography: Jim Allen

Macmillan Canada
An imprint of CDG Books Canada Inc.
Toronto

Printed in Canada

DEDICATION

To my nephews,
Michael, Paul, Joel, and Adam
and to the next generation,
my great-niece and -nephew,
Tovah and Noah

A joyful future

ACKNOWLEDGEMENTS

O*nly you can do it, but you can't do it alone*. This book was created with the wisdom and help of many people. My gratitude and deep appreciation to:

Bernie Klein, my "cheerleader," for his love and support. My (tea) cup runneth over with joy!

My agent, Michael Levine, for his expert guidance and legal counsel, and to Arne Fors, trademark specialist.

Jennifer Glossop, my patient editor, for her wisdom and continual encouragement to keep writing.

Dina Ruffle, my right and left arm, who performs double duty looking after our chiropractic clinic, as well as my book and public-speaking engagements.

David Talbot, caring friend and mentor, who started me on my path to authordom.

A special thank you to all the exceptional older adults who use the good dishes: Doris Anderson, Rabbi Bernard Baskin, Mary Bourn, June Callwood, Judge Roger Conant, Henry Den Braber, Libby Dwor, Ralph Farrell, Paul Giroux, Helen Gougeon, Grace Irwin, Chancellor Henry Jackman, Gert Kushin, Allen Lambert, Jay Lipsey, Judge Hugh Locke, Doris McCarthy, Judge Bill MacLatchy, Helen McLean, Sylvia Molson, the late Faye Mosoff, Dr. Marie Murphy, Phil Nimmons, Deirdre O'Connell, Ben Orenstein, Iris Peterson, Phyllis Pilgrim, Major General Richard Rohmer, Mickey Rooney, Dr. Robert Salter, Hope Sealy, Ethel Scholl, Deborah Szekely, Mary Thomas, Helen and John Weinzweig, Doreen and Ben Wicks, Don Wright, and Joe Womersley.

And thank you to all those who shared their expertise with me, including Dr. Dan Baker, Dr. Lawrence Ballon, Dr. Howard Book, Barbara Burrows, Dr. Deepak Chopra, Roger Gabriel,

Dr. Harry Hardin, Reesa Kassirer MSW, Dr. Pam Letts, Kye (Carol) Marshall, Anne Parker, Shelley Stein MSW, Dr. Judy Turner, and Carol Wise.

My sincere appreciation for sharing their personal stories with me to Sharon Allen, Brenda and Gary Baker, Pat Bartlett-Richards, Mory Baxter, Bobby Beder, Robert Brissenden, Steve Burns, Pearl Cassel, Denise Cherrington, Anne Cowie, Robert Craig, Earl Crangle, Sule Gjoca, Erica Glossop, Ellen Foster, Robert Gage, Wendy Harris, Carol Hayes, Carl Hiebert, Bryant Kassirer, the late Charlotte Klein, Danny Klein, Andrea Kraus, Darlene Lamb, Henry Less, Terri Licalzi, Gerry Lokash, Linda Markowsky, D'Arcy Martin, Gordon McClellan, Robert Munsch, Sharon Newman, Carol Peterson, Candice Rice, Barbara Rosenberg, Alan Schwartz, Maureen Sheedy, Candice Sheldon, Penny Shore, Rifka Silverberg, Gerda Sippert, Joseph Sorbara, Reva Stern, Dr. Janet Tamo, Penny Thomsen, Joe Thompson, Kai Whalley, and Bernie Younder.

My gratitude for their help to Judge Denise Bellamy, Michael Burgess, Wendy Cecil-Cockwell, Sidney Cohen, Penny Fine, Bertha Madott, Liz Manore, Rona Maynard, Donna Messer, Valerie Pringle, Marv Schrieder, Ruth Stern, and Irene Wright.

Once again, I am thrilled to be working with the team at CDG Books Canada (under the Macmillan imprint). Special thanks to my editor, Jennifer Lambert, who is a delight to work with. My sincere appreciation to Hart Hillman and Robert Harris for believing in this project. Thanks also to Sara James, Anna Stancer, Brian Cartwright, and Jennifer Smith.

My appreciation to photographer Jim Allen and graphic designer Gillian Tsintziras for their creative genius.

And, especially, thank you to my dear family, which has grown since I wrote *Passionate Longevity*, for their love and encouragement: Cheryl and Steven, Joel, Adam, Paul and Jennifer, and Michael and Julie—parents of my godchild and great-niece, Tovah, and baby Noah, my great-nephew.

Contents

USE THE GOOD DISHES™

Use the good dishes; what are you waiting for?
Putting life on hold, hoping for something more?
I'll tell you when is good: good is every day.
Look at the millions of people who didn't wake up today.
I'll bet they'd trade a day for every one we waste.
Pretend you've got a year to live,
wouldn't you then make haste?
To tell those close you love them, and cherish them so much,
Your friends who have been there for you,
all the lives you've touched.
Would you notice puffy clouds, hear birds,
and smell the flowers?
Climb a mountain, sing and dance,
look for rainbows after the showers?
Forgive someone who's hurt you?
What about the things you've done?
Do you need to say I'm sorry to a parent, a child, or someone
That you meant to spend some time with,
but stuff got in the way?
Oh well, there's always tomorrow, or maybe some other day.
I'll be happy when—I'll be happy if I met the right one,
Or when I'm retired, or my mortgage is paid.
Soon I'll have some fun.
The beauty of life is the journey,
all the day-to-day lessons we learn.
Be grateful for the rough ones, the pain and the tough ones,
everyone has their turn.
Each day is a gift; it's a present we should be most thankful for.
Open it now! Don't save it. We never know what's in store.
"One of these days" is here now. Don't look back with regret.
When you live, laugh, and love,
the good dishes on the table of life you have set.

INTRODUCTION

This is my mission statement, printed in large bold letters, framed, and hung on my office wall: My purpose in life is to touch the lives of others with my positive energy. Since 1995, with the release and subsequent success of my first book, *Passionate Longevity: The 10 Secrets to Growing Younger*, I have been living that mission—grateful to be motivating and inspiring audiences everywhere. Doors opened, allowing me to speak to thousands of people—mostly baby boomers like me—who have more than just a passing interest in longevity. Forget Toys 'R' Us; when you reach that milestone called the big 5–0, Aging 'R' Us! With that comes an acute awareness of the acceleration of time. When I began writing *Passionate Longevity*, I was 44. My youngest nephews were kids; now they're teenagers talking about their plans for university. My brother Steven, at 53, is *kvelling* (gushing) over Tovah and Noah, the newest joys in our growing family, making him a grandfather and me a doting great-aunt.

As we age, all of us receive an inevitable wake-up call, the death of a family member, a friend, or (for me) a patient. Perhaps this increased sense of mortality explains the reaction I received two years ago when I blurted out, "Use the good dishes," during a speech. The audience greeted that line with great laughter and applause. And since then every time I've said it the response is the same. Somehow those four words capture the essence of what we know at 50: Life must be celebrated every day.

Several months after introducing that phrase, I sat down and wrote a poem entitled "Use the Good Dishes," expressing what those four words meant to me. My thoughts flowed: ...*good is every day...pretend you've got a year to live...the beauty of life is the journey…each day is a gift…"one of these days" is here now—don't look back with regret.* Then one day I was listening to the radio when the host announced an upcoming program about dealing with loss, prompted by the untimely death of Princess Diana. I faxed him my poem, which he read on the air. Our office received over 200 telephone calls requesting copies. More than 5000 copies of the poem have now been sold in poster form.

Writing a poem, however, didn't qualify me as an expert on how to *live* the message. Besides, my good dishes were still displayed behind glass buffet doors! So for guidance, I decided to revisit older adults whose wisdom has already mentored me through the past six years of my journey through life. I realized that, at 50, I was ready for more lessons to prepare me for the next leg of the trip. My journey up to now has taken me through loss into a relationship, from questions about health and longevity to questions about values and happiness. My search for answers to life's deepest questions led me to the hearts and minds of 40 wise "life mentors." When I asked them what "use the good dishes" meant to them, their answers touched me deeply. Small, ordinary, everyday things are the joy in our life, they told me. Don't wait for big things to make you happy. Be conscious, awake. Pay attention and you will notice the smell of fresh-cut grass. Feel the warmth of the sun on your face. Stop and listen to the rhythmic melody of a cardinal singing to a mate. Care about people; give gifts of time, friendship, and love. Be silly; laugh and play with children and animals. Simplify your life; say no when you need to; let go and trust the universe. Treasure the rituals and happy memories in your life. Decorate your fridge door or the walls with photos of people you love. Live in the "living room." With courage, colour outside the lines of your life so that you don't merely exist; explore, risk, and live life like an exclamation mark! Never take one day for granted; be grateful that you woke up at all.

Learn to love the process of life and detach yourself from the outcome. Touch someone's spirit; hold hands, listen, be there—for family, friends, or a stranger. Care about the planet, our home.

I soon began to ask everyone I know—young and old—this question: *How do you find joy in everyday life?* Hundreds of people shared their most special tiny pleasures. You can read their poignant replies throughout the book. You will also understand what tugs at my heart. Meet "The Boogeyman," visit my "Fridge Door," discover "Rekindlegarten"—to name a few of my poems in this book.

We know that life works in mysterious yet meaningful ways. Somehow it wasn't sufficient to just *ask* others how they use the good dishes. The universe decided that the only way for me to be an authority on the subject is through personal experience; as you read this book you will understand that I am living this phrase fully, from the inside out.

I hope that this book will provide a map for baby boomers who are now ready to journey on a more insightful path. But before you begin reading, rip the plastic off the couches, then curl up on the sofa with a cup of tea in your Royal Doulton teacup.

May your table of life always be set with good dishes filled with love, equanimity, and joy!

ADAPTING

Baby Boomer Rap

Listen, baby boomers, to what I have to say:
Your body is aging with each passing day.
Your muscles and joints feel stiff and tight.
Discs are thinning. You're losing your height.
Hairline's receding and so are your gums.
A touch of sciatica, a leg goes numb.
Increasing wrinkles and greying hair,
A new lump or bump can give you a scare.
Check out the prostate if you're a guy.
Deaths from heart disease, way too high.
Women have their problems, that's because
Of osteoporosis and menopause.
We need orthotics for fallen arches,
Watch that cholesterol, more veggies and starches.
Memory loss and constipation,
Impotence and eyesight deterioration.
When you're over 50, injuries heal slow,
Like plantar fasciitis and tennis elbow.
Sometimes pessimistic, can get depressed,
You feel the years are fleeting and full of stress.

Listen, baby boomers, to what I have to say:
Look and feel great, just follow my way.
Keep your body moving, can't be fit if you sit.
Follow good nutrition, and supplement it.
Stretch and tone those muscles, you'll move with ease.

A smoke- and drug-free body means less disease.
Work at what you love, and laugh each day.
Nourish your mind, don't forget to play.
Cherish your family, be a good friend.
A good night's sleep helps the body mend.
Love in your heart, compassion in your soul.
Help someone younger reach their goal.
Find joy in small everyday things,
A flower, a book, silence, or sing.
There's a healthy way to age, you can pursue.
Getting better not older, it's up to you.

MAKING PEACE

I feel smug. I just discovered I'm the oldest person in my exercise class, a tortuous high-intensity one-hour workout of hill climbing and racing on a sturdy stationary bike. Surrounded by a group of fit 20-, 30-, and a handful of 40-year-olds, this 51-year-old can keep pace with the best of them. Of course, by the time I show up for class, I've already pushed my muscles through a vigorous one-hour weight-training program. Some may ask why I've changed my routine, especially those who remember me as a runner first. Call it dealing with reality or adapting to change. Just don't think of it as the dreaded aging process!

Three years ago I had to make a major adjustment in my fitness regime. A sharp pain in my left foot was diagnosed as a stress fracture. The cumulative effects of pounding the pavement over two decades of distance running coupled with lousy biomechanics had weakened my foot. Dembe's rule one: Rest the injured part to facilitate healing. Dembe's rule two: Find an alternative to maintain your fitness level and sanity. Initially I intended to join a club for only three months, just long enough to switch to a non-weight-bearing exercise, heal my foot, and then go back to running.

How do you find joy in everyday life?

However, once my eyes were opened to the huge variety of fitness activities available, I stopped depending on running alone to keep me in shape. This is where Dembe's rule three comes in: Sometimes when we are forced to shift gears, we emerge happier and healthier than we were before. For example, I never bothered with weight training when I was just running. Now I have incorporated strength work into my aerobic program three times per week, because muscle mass decreases after age 50. I've also improved my flexibility by taking the time to stretch my muscles before exercising.

I am now back to running five miles once or twice a week, and have noticed a positive change in my outlook. I don't really care how slowly I run or how long it takes me to complete a particular route. In fact, I don't wear a watch any more. While time, distance, and speed used to be my mantra, I am now more concerned with staying healthy and vital for the rest of my life. I remember wondering as a child why my parents would always toast to "good health," thinking that being healthy was as normal as breathing. Now I know why. At 51, I realize more than ever that to a large extent health is the result of the lifestyle choices we make. Obviously, genetics play a role, too. Plus, it helps to have a smattering of luck and maybe a guardian angel or two to keep us out of harm's way.

Something happens at around 50: You finally begin to make peace with the body you are given. I no longer sigh with envy while looking at magazines with supermodels strutting their tight butts in thong underwear. Now that I am on my "third box of birthday candles" (there are 24 in a box!) I accept that (a) I'll never be a supermodel and (b) I have spider veins, bunions, a few wrinkles, some brown spots, receding gums, and I'm okay with it. After asking a stranger in the supermarket to help me decipher the blurred printing on a package, I decided to consult an optometrist. I now wear prescription glasses, which is the most recent change I'm adapting to.

I meditate for 30 minutes in the morning.

Pat, artist

I boasted to psychotherapist Shelley Stein that I feel a wonderful sense of self-acceptance at 51 with the admission that I am not perfect. She wisely shot back, "That means you are making a judgement about what is perfect." She was right. "Just accept, *period*," she said firmly. "This is me, this is who I am. Everyone is perfect. There is a perfect them. We are who we are. We need to accept and love ourselves and then choose to make certain behavioural, lifestyle, and emotional changes without changing who we essentially are."

Many of my patients are baby boomers who, like me, are coming to terms with mid-life and aging issues. Let's face it: Aging sneaks in the back door while we are living life. At mid-life, we must come to terms with two realities: we are not immortal, and loss is inevitable. We may have already experienced major losses, such as the death of a parent, the end of a marriage or significant relationship, a job or career termination, or a change in our physical health. Unfortunately we also understand that as we age, others age with us, so there are more losses yet to come.

I consulted with psychiatrist Dr. Howard Book, who shared his expertise on adapting. "We must adapt the way we think, feel, and behave to changing situations and circumstances," he believes. "A component of adapting is acceptance—the ability to acknowledge our strengths and weaknesses and feel good about ourselves nonetheless." In order to adapt to life's changes, we have to know ourselves. Explains Dr. Book, "We have to be familiar with how we are. If we have a pattern of behaviour, thoughts, and feelings to a given situation and the situation changes, unless we're aware of what that pattern is, we won't be able to shift. If we don't know, for example, that our body is not the same at 65 as it was at 35 and we continue to push ourselves to run or lift weights as hard, we will damage ourselves. If we are aware that our body is changing, we can adapt and shift our behaviour and still remain physically healthy while accepting our limitations."

For some, accepting our limitations means changing the way

I look in the mirror while I'm shaving and thank God that I'm strong and able to continue my life the way it has been.

George, businessman

we think about our bodies. We must recognize that we cannot control every aspect of what happens to us. How do we adapt when life hands us physical challenges? The following story may give you an idea.

Every May at my house, three skylights, streaked with bird droppings, have a date with the energetic arms of my favourite window washer. I call this "dirty dancing with Bill." For the past 26 years he has cleaned millions of panes of glass. "I reach all the obscure areas where birds love to leave their calling cards and cleaning ladies fear to tread," he laughed. "I sometimes dream that if I could collect all the ladder rungs I've climbed over the years and make one long continuous ladder, it would stretch right up to heaven. I could have coffee with God!"

Bill is friendly—a happy-go-lucky kind of guy with a crooked smile that ends where a deep scar begins, in a criss-cross pattern that meanders over his lower lip, chin, and neck. When I met him 13 years ago, I thought that he might have been attacked by a knife-wielding thug, but I never asked. It was none of my business. We chatted briefly last spring and I told him the title of the book I was writing.

"Hmm," he muttered, pursing his scarred lips. "I definitely use the good dishes—*now*."

"So what changed?" I pushed gently, aware of his emphasis on the word *now*. His story spilled out:

Fifteen years ago Bill went to his family doctor with what he thought was an infection on his lower lip. The doctor mistakenly diagnosed a cold sore and Bill left with medication. A month passed, with no improvement. Bill was then sent to a plastic surgeon at the local hospital for a biopsy. A terrible infection followed and Bill was hospitalized for eight days. "I ended up having three more surgeries and skin grafts. My lip did not heal." He decided to get another opinion at a hospital. Bill was diagnosed with squamous cell carcinoma, which by that time had spread to his neck. "I had to endure 13 hours of face and neck surgery to

I get up an hour before the rest of the family (including the dog) for quiet time to organize my day.

Ingrid, teacher

remove the tumour, followed by 28 horrible radiation treatments; then I needed reconstructive surgery of my lower chin, lip, and neck. My face resembled a pizza with eight wedges neatly sliced out. I was a mess, but thankful to be alive."

Bill could have been bitter, angry, or litigious. Instead, he learned some valuable lessons. "I now realize what's really important in life," he nodded thoughtfully. "And it's not how someone looks. Forget my scars. I'm a human being with feelings!" he exclaimed. "And all those homeowners' possessions—the fancy furniture and good dishes that I can see through the glass—don't mean much if you hate the person you're living with. I can hear couples fighting! I've also learned to make the best of each day and never take a new one for granted. I don't let little things bug me any more, like if someone cuts me off in traffic. Hey, I'm a survivor!" he laughed. "You know what song I whistle when I'm washing windows? 'Grey skies are gonna clear up, put on a happy face!'"

Bill taught me much about accepting what is. Then I learned from Arthur an even more powerful lesson about resourcefulness, which Dr. Book feels is a vital component of being adaptive. Here is what happened on a recent flight from Tampa to Toronto:

Air Canada flight 905 was almost full. I hoped that if someone sat next to me it would be an exhausted adult who didn't feel like talking. I planned to immerse myself in a silent cloud of creativity, to finish a poem on touch and holding hands. After about a dozen passengers filed past my seat, a man stopped, smiled, and slipped in beside me. Meet Arthur, 54, a lawyer from the east coast. Nice enough, I sensed, and we began to chat. He had been visiting his elderly parents who were winter residents in Florida. It didn't take me long to give him my life story, albeit abbreviated. Never wanting to miss an opportunity, I had to tell him about my first book (and I just happened to have a copy in my carry-on bag and would be delighted to autograph it for him and his wife). Then I recited "Use the Good Dishes." Buoyed by his enthusiasm, I read him the rough draft of the new poem I had been working

When I wake up in the morning, I thank God for returning my soul, and then I kiss all the family photos sitting on my dresser and wish everyone a good day.

Gert, mother

on. He nodded thoughtfully, but didn't seem very inspired. And that's when I noticed that Arthur had no fingers on his left hand! There I was writing a poem about holding hands and the universe conspired to remind me, with a strong dose of reality, that not everyone is as fortunate as I am.

Arthur was born with a congenital birth defect whereby the bones in his fingers did not fuse properly. To correct the problem, the doctors simply removed his fingers. He was left with only a palm and a thumb.

I asked him how he coped with this, thinking of all the functions that fingers perform.

He answered me frankly. "The hardest thing was learning how to tie my shoelaces. At first I had to ask my mom to do it for me. The best feeling in the world was on the day I could actually tie them by myself. I was ten years old."

I hesitated, then, thinking about my poem. Finally, I ventured, "What about holding hands?"

"Well," he began, "my teenage years were rough. I was very self-conscious. People always stared at my left hand, but never mentioned anything about it, almost pretending my deformity didn't exist. I didn't have many girlfriends. In fact, I don't remember ever holding hands with anyone except the girl who became my wife. I met her when I was 23. Thankfully, she was a nurse. She said to me, 'It's no big deal,' and that was that. She never made an issue of it."

When the plane landed I watched as Arthur reached down with his right hand to grab his luggage. Then he stopped. He looked me right in the eye and said, "You are one of the few people who has ever asked me how I really feel living with this disability. I want to thank you for that."

With a lump in my throat I replied, "And, Arthur, thank you for teaching me one of life's special lessons." I reached for his left hand, held it for a moment, and said goodbye. He had touched me more than he knew.

Every day I kibitz with people to make them laugh.
                                        Victor, entrepreneur

JOINT FLEXIBILITY

I was recently joking with a patient about aging as I searched for my glasses to make a note in her file. "The world got blurry the instant I turned 50," I told her. She laughed, but then expressed some concern about her 79-year-old husband. "I'm starting to get worried about John's short-term memory loss," she confided. I've known this delightful couple for about 12 years. She is active, healthy, and 16 years younger than he is. Her husband, who is retired, has had cancer. "I told him this morning that I had an appointment with you and he had forgotten by the afternoon. I get annoyed with him more and more, as I have to keep reminding him about so many things."

At mid-life and beyond, the rules change. The initial contract that we agreed upon as a couple acquires addenda as we age. Health changes are only one aspect of what we must adapt to. Career challenges, retirement, and the empty-nest syndrome all affect how a couple relates to each other. In simple terms, if you've been doing the waltz with your partner for 30 years, and suddenly you want to learn hip hop, both of you need to talk about the changes to the program. Psychotherapist Dr. Judy Turner, co-author of *The Healthy Boomer*, agrees. "As a couple grows older together, the relationship that they originally signed onto is not the same as it's going to be 20 years from now. Let's say a man has traditionally been the breadwinner and the woman has stayed home. Now in mid-life, the man wants to do more nurturing things and the woman wants to make her mark in the business world. They change as individuals and they change in terms of what being a couple now means to them. It's important to work things out at a friendship level. If they can't adapt, then their relationship will be in trouble."

Statistics tell us that the world's population is aging. On an individual basis we are living longer, healthier lives. We have time to do a lot more in our lives. Gone are the days when we

Every Saturday I call my sister who lives in England.
                            Lillian, homemaker

worked in one career until we retired, then died. Now many are leaving their primary work at an early age with vitality and ener-gy to start something new, with a third to a half of their life spans ahead of them. Mid-life change in one partner affects the other. One of my patients quit an executive position that gave him end-less perks and moved to a life of self-employment in his home office using the Internet. He and his wife had to adapt to a different social status, as well as to increased togetherness during the day. As long as couples understand each other's needs and wishes, they can pursue different avenues. When you share your dreams with your partner, you can in time develop a plan that considers both of your needs.

One of my patients fell into a depression after the youngest of her three children left home for college. So much of her life revolved around her family that she had made no provisions for her own future or for the changing dynamic with her husband. Most of their conversations focused on the children. "In the beginning I had to rehearse in my mind what we would talk about at dinner. I realized to an extent that this man was a stranger to me. He agreed to joint therapy and the therapist recommended getting a puppy, as I still needed someone who depended on me. Walking the dog together was the glue that bonded us again."

About a year ago, a man came into my office complaining of neck pain. Two weeks earlier, he had lost his corporate executive position as a result of downsizing, and I concluded that his prob-lem was mostly stress-related. His wife, a homemaker looking after three children, was forced to find a job. Frustrated by being at home for some time, she had no notion of what she wanted to do. I recently saw him and learned how he and his wife successfully adapted to the role reversal. "We talked about how we could make this new situation work for both of us," he told me. "She decided to study for her real estate licence and I agreed to stay at home and look after the kids. I had to learn to accept her as a working woman and she had to accept the fact that I would run the house.

I love listening to music on my CD player while I drive.
Bernie, entrepreneur

She is doing quite well in real estate now, and frankly, after driving myself hard for 25 years, I am enjoying the break from the competitive world. I've got a regular fitness routine, I'm not a bad cook, and my woodworking hobby may turn into a little business. I've been making doll cribs, and trucks for kids. I've got a few orders for Christmas, so you never know where it will end up!"

The healthiest, happiest people keep growing and learning their entire life. They are able to adapt to change, recognizing that it can open up new horizons, physically, emotionally, and spiritually. It follows, then, that they can accept the same process in their partners. Communicating, in a supportive way, will allow a relationship in the midst of transition to continue to blossom with true intimacy, companionship, and love.

ANCHORED IN REALITY

I have a drawing that inspires me. It shows a man standing on the pinnacle of a mountain, hand outstretched, grabbing a star right out of the sky. I am reminded of the poetry of Robert Browning: "Ah, but a man's reach should exceed his grasp, or what's a heaven for?" My hands have been reaching skyward for as long as I can remember, fuelled by a burning passion to make a difference in the world. When I was 12, my dreams and wishes were like amorphous clouds floating in a sky of infinite possibilities. My expectations then were as lofty as the heavens. Now, decades later, still bursting with hopes and dreams, my expectations have been tempered by a more realistic view of life. Usually by the time we reach 50, we have collected some wisdom to help us adapt and learn from our experiences. Disappointment can also be an effective anchor—a way to bring one's feet back down to the ground.

Expectation is the anticipation of an outcome and the wish that it will happen. We have expectations about our day, our partners,

I love singing along to songs on the radio, especially the "oldies" when I know most of the words.

Joanne, office manager

and how our life is going to be. Individuals carry thousands of trivial expectations in their minds every day. We expect that we will wake up in the morning. When we open the front door, we expect our newspapers to be there. We need expectations to give our day structure and to help us organize for tomorrow. We plan our future around our expectations. We could not save money for retirement, plan a vacation, or winterize our homes without anticipating the future.

Unrealistic expectations, however, can get us into trouble, particularly when it involves relationships, work, family, and ourselves. I asked Dr. Judy Turner whether dreaming about an anticipated outcome sets us up for disappointment. She laughed and said, "It depends if you are awake or asleep!" She believes that we need to achieve a balance between reaching beyond and reality. "If you learn to play the piano at 50 and expect to play at Carnegie Hall at 55, you are going to be disappointed. Expectations must be tempered with the acceptance of limitations of ourselves and others." Dr. Turner counsels clients who often have unrealistic expectations in their relationships. "A client might say to me, 'My husband seemed so wonderful, so perfect.' Our perception of people often gets coloured by our expectations. If clients have chronic cycles of big expectations followed by disappointments, we need to look at their attitudes as well as the degree of realism reflected in their expectations."

Recently a patient complained of stress-related shoulder pain. While probing his issues as well as his tissues, I discovered that his computer organizer contained a daily to-do list that even the president of the United States, aided by numerous staff, would find daunting. His expectations of what he could accomplish each day were out of sync with reality and set him up for failure. To make matters worse, unfinished projects were carried over for months, creating an infinite list of impossibilities. His self-defeating behaviour reminded me of the story of Sisyphus, the Greek mortal who was condemned by the gods to ceaselessly push a rock

I call my 84-year-old mother who lives in Newfoundland, just to hear her voice.

Doreen, store owner

to the top of a mountain, whereupon the stone would roll back down. I explained to him that he was carrying the burden of unmet expectations on his shoulders. Unless he adjusted his expectations accordingly and set priorities, he would continue to feel disappointed, stressed, and joyless. He began to understand that the delete button on his computer could very well be his best friend. Then I told him about my own to-do list. I keep my expectations low so I can reward myself daily. Only exaggerating slightly, I told him that "eat breakfast" and "show up at the office" are on my to-do list!

It is difficult enough to meet one's own expectations. What about those individuals who grew up believing that they had to be perfect for their parents to love them or approve of them? Psychotherapist Shelley Stein explained the consequences of unrealistic demands and expectations from parents. "Children see themselves through their parents' eyes. Regardless of how old we are, we carry that child within us. If the early messages from our parents were focused on unattainable goals, we tend to internalize those expectations. This results in endless striving to achieve something that is continually beyond our grasp."

"Does this play a role in perfectionism?" I asked her. "Absolutely," she replied. "Perfectionists have difficulty in completing tasks. They become immobilized by the fear of not achieving perfection." She cited the case of a graduate student who could not complete his thesis because it was not perfect enough. Shelley helps clients by asking them to see the situation happening to someone else. "Perfectionists have a double standard. They are too hard on themselves yet quite forgiving and accepting of others doing the same thing. I ask them to look at the inappropriateness of their belief system. They must learn to question the negative messages they received from parents, teachers, and other influences."

Relationships can be problematic when there is, in Shelley Stein's words, "romantic perfectionism," or unrealistic expectations

Every morning after I feed Kitty, she profusely thanks me with meows and brushes her body back and forth across my shins.

Paul, chef

of the other person. A new romance can send us into the realm of fantasy and illusion. With the passing of time, we get to know the other person, and gain a more realistic perspective. (Yes, that perfect man *does* snore and forget to bring you flowers on your birthday!) Many couples do not share their expectations with each other, often leading to frustration and disappointment in a relationship. David Talbot, a lifestyle coach, counselled an engaged couple who came to his office to plan their future. "Verbalizing openly what they expected for themselves and each other seemed to be the glue that cemented their relationship." Judge Bill MacLatchy, age 70, agrees that a significant cause of unhappiness is unrealistic expectations in a relationship. MacLatchy, who for years has presided over family and matrimonial cases, believes, "You must accommodate and adapt to the needs of your partner. It boils down to selfishness. People put their own wishes and desires ahead of the other person in a partnership. You can't do that." He should know. Happily married for 48 years to Joyce, he gets the greatest joy from nurturing and giving to others. "Every weekend while Joyce sleeps in, I get up and make her the best raisin, cinnamon, and nutmeg oatmeal for breakfast. Joyce does so much for me, looking after my life in great style. Again, it is your outlook and realistic expectations that are important."

So how do we maintain a balance between reality and illusion and minimize the frequency of disappointments in our life? We need to be flexible, believes psychiatrist Dr. Howard Book. "Turning 50 changes our perspective. No longer is it an all-promising, anything-is-possible future. We have to accept that there are limitations. Wisdom is the ability to view things as they are objectively, rather than the way we wish them to be." But let me inject a note of optimism here. If we walk around thinking of staying within our self-imposed limitations, we'll be reluctant to try anything new, to dream, to reach for that star. Let's return for a moment to Dr. Judy Turner's example of learning to play the piano at 50. Who cares if you don't get to Carnegie Hall? What is important

I make funny faces and laugh in the mirror and that automatically puts a smile on my face.

Danny, professor

is the personal satisfaction of trying to play the piano in the first place. It doesn't matter whether we will be *good* at it, because the best reason for doing anything is that it brings us joy.

And that means approaching expectations without attachment. When we invest too heavily in any one outcome (the eggs-in-one-basket principle) we set ourselves up for disappointment. Hairdresser Robert Gage says he is hard to disappoint because he doesn't count on things to work out in a certain way. "I have learned to detach myself from the outcome of everything. I know what I want, but I don't put myself in a position to plan exactly how this day is going to go. That is like living life with the brakes on. For me, living life without expectation means I am enjoying the trip and not focusing on the destination." D'Arcy Martin now lives the same way as Robert. "I used to have very lofty goals, always striving to reach them. Then I realized that I was getting too clingy, too invested in a specific result or outcome. I would push myself and others in unreasonable ways that generated resentment from them and frustration in me. In the last four years I've become disengaged from outcomes, trusting more in the process." And when we learn to trust the process, we are more accepting when we don't get what we wanted or expected. We are more philosophical, understanding that life is unfolding as it should.

As I type this sentence, New Year's—the big Millennium Bash 2000—is about a month away. For the past 12 months, we've been deluged with suggestions as to how to make this once-in-a-century blowout a spectacular night. I ask you: Could anyone's New Year's live up to the hype, to the high expectations set by the media? I guarantee that when many of us wake up on January 1, 2000, we will say, "Is that all there is?" As you read this now, think about how your New Year's was. Were you disappointed? In the past, have you frequently had high expectations of an event that was impossibly idealistic? Your fiftieth birthday party? A special vacation? Every disappointment is an opportunity for us to re-evaluate, to get a reading on how well we have assessed the

---

I speak to a different friend every day—no business talk—we just laugh, tell jokes, check in with each other.

Jeffrey, entertainment producer

reality of a situation. Those individuals who admit they are too hard on themselves should follow psychotherapist Shelley Stein's suggestion: "Give yourself permission to renegotiate the rules. Ask yourself: Do I need to be doing this? Is it reasonable to expect that after working all day, one must make dinner every single night for the family? Accept that you are human, which means that we are not perfect and we make mistakes. Look at the limiting beliefs that cause you stress."

If we see it in an optimistic way, disappointment can be a friend, an ally in our search for a joyful life. It can motivate us to learn from our negative and painful experiences. When we respond to disappointment in a positive and hopeful manner, we will come to understand this: While food may not always taste better on the good dishes, you will still feel more joyful when you're eating from them.

Grown—Alone!

I once was a we, but now that he
Did flee with she—I'm a me!
I'm a free and happy divorcee.
Initially I was feeling lonely,
I'd hesitate to say, "Table for one."
Shy and reclusive, not ready for fun,
Girlfriends and family really pulled me through.
Some well-meaning friends tried to rescue
With a few blind dates—not first rate.
I'd rather hibernate.
But that was then and this is now;
I knew I'd get through that phase somehow.
I had to learn a new comfort zone.

Taking Lulu, my dog, for the last walk of the day at night means my day is over and I can completely relax and go to bed.

Robert, hairdresser

Now content to live on my own,
It's the only way I have really grown—alone—
A milestone!
If you're living alone, I recommend
You learn to be your own best friend.
Society thinks if you're looking good
There must be a man—that's a falsehood!
You can be happy alone and in my view
I'd rather be a one than an unhappy two
Who's just making do; if you value you,
Don't pursue.

I figured out what single life's about:
It's not deprivation or doing without.
Don't have to close the bathroom door.
Your clothes are where you left them—
On the floor.
Don't have to cook fancy—eat soup from the pot.
I can binge on chocolate and not get caught.
Forget to brush your teeth? Well, who really cares?
Your dog and cat still love you—you should smell theirs!
You really save time making half the bed.
No loud obnoxious snoring near your head.
Don't have to put down the toilet seat.
You can make natural noises, when food repeats.
You can squish the toothpaste any way you feel.
Groceries cost less, boy, what a deal!
Pick a movie of your choice and see it alone.
Never liked to share popcorn, I've always known.

The life I live is one of choice, not chance.
Don't get me wrong, I'm open for romance.
If it happens it happens, I'm not really looking.

I love watching my child's face when she's sleeping.
                                        Susan, mother

Can make the whole bed, don't mind extra cooking,
Or putting down the toilet seat.
Gets cold in winter, need extra body heat.
Can be quite flexible, I'll wear earplugs
If he starts to snore; it's worth the hugs
And the loving and the sharing and the caring I get.
When two people are in love, it's the best and yet
I've had it with and without and without a doubt
I've been in and out, either raining or a drought.
I know what love's about, so look out!
What's really changed is my attitude.
Life's lessons I'm learning with gratitude.
Live today with a smile, curious for tomorrow—
Happy and alive, got no time for sorrow!

Writing this poem in 1992 was a victory for me. I finally conquered the "needy stage" that occurs after a relationship ends. I triumphantly adapted to my divorce in two not-so-easy steps: from twosome to lonesome, finally graduating to onesome. With therapy, my lifeline of family and friends, an optimistic spirit, and acceptance, I learned that life was unfolding as it should. Now, 11 years later, I've gone from messed up to blissed out, as I am happily ensconced in a relationship with a wonderful guy! I have a theory about that: I believe that the universe decided to wait until I became whole—emotionally ready and content on my own—before surprising me with Bernie.

At mid-life and beyond, living alone by choice or by circumstance is common—whether you are single, divorced, or widowed. For every one person who lives alone happily, there are two stuck somewhere in between lonely and if only. Widower Jay Lipsey, a vital man in his mid-nineties, would like to have a companion in his life. "I'd like to embrace someone and I'm sure I'd enjoy it. I know quite a few ladies but I just haven't met anyone who has charmed me." His wife died in 1982 after 53 years of

I love the feeling that I get after doing my daily 40-minute cardiovascular exercise, knowing, once it's behind me, that I can relax and get on with the rest of my day.

                                                    Robert, hairdresser

marriage, then three years later he fell in love with a woman who also died. "Two losses in three years is too much," Jay said sadly. "I'm still not over it. I feel like a jigsaw puzzle with a piece missing. But I have to accept it, that's all."

Deirdre O'Connell, 82, describes herself as single and interested in life. Never married, this former reporter and information writer is busy taking courses in history, music, and art and enjoys close friendships. "Romantic love is a bonus if it comes," she said. "Often marriage doesn't work out because people marry for the wrong reasons—their friends are marrying or time urgency pressures them into marriage."

I understand from my own personal experience that each of us has the choice to interpret a major life event in a way that either makes us stronger or incapacitates us. For Libby Dwor, 84, the process was quite straightforward after her husband died. "I had a very happy marriage. Once I made up my mind that I wasn't going to remarry, my life became very easy." Independent is how I would describe Libby, who knows how to enjoy her own company. "I don't mind doing things by myself. If I want to hear a lecture and no one wants to go, I'll take a cab and go myself. I never deny myself the pleasure of doing something just because I have no one to go with."

Music educator Don Wright, now 90, married his sweetheart, Lillian Meighen, in 1935. They shared a special relationship for almost 58 years, until she died in 1993. On his curriculum vitae he wrote, "My wife, Lillian, was my indispensable partner and inspiring companion in all my endeavours. Her constant help and encouragement stimulated me through the years." How has Don coped with living alone? "I am grateful for everything that's happened to me, good and bad," he said. "The bad things taught me some damn good life lessons. I talk to my Lillybelle every day, which is a great comfort to me."

Journalist Helen Gougeon learned an important life lesson about living alone. When she was 56, her husband died at age

I sit alone in a coffee shop reading the current issue of Gourmet magazine.

Aileen, mother of two

74. One year later she married again. "Too quickly," she admitted. "I was delaying my grief." Now 76, she can look back and say with certainty, "I know now I would have been okay living on my own." Her second husband died a few years later, after they had separated. Helen then found what some may call the perfect arrangement. "In 1988 I reconnected with someone else, who lived in New Brunswick. I would arrive in beautiful St. Andrews in late spring to be with him and stay to the end of the summer, then he would spend winters in Toronto with me. In between we took a hiatus. This lasted for ten years. It was not a daily love relationship." I laughed when Helen recounted a particular response to an article she was writing on what makes an ideal relationship. One woman replied, "I'd like to be married on weekends and holidays!"

When artist Doris McCarthy was 37, she fell in love with a married man, and hoped that the relationship would lead to marriage. After seven years she ended the affair. "You get your lessons when you're ready for them," she said matter-of-factly. This 89-year-old has been living on her own ever since. How has she adapted? "I am in many love relationships. I could not live alone without love in my life. Many people have not learned to like themselves well enough to enjoy living alone. I like myself. I'm good company and I'm happy."

CHOOSING HARMONY

One of the basic tenets of life is that nothing ever remains the same. Life is constantly evolving and we must adapt to it. We all know individuals who thrive in the face of change and others who rigidly resist.

Libby Dwor, 84, is a prime example of someone who chose synergy over struggle through her optimistic approach to life. Her inspiring story begins when she was a young bride living in Port

I buy fresh flowers in the winter.

Jennifer, editor

Colbourne, Ontario, with her husband, Richard, and his mother, Bubba. "I knew before I was married that Richard's mother would be living with us," Libby recalled. "He told me that he wouldn't marry anyone, regardless of how much he loved them, if they didn't accept his mother. I could have interpreted this in two ways: This marriage is not going to work because he is so tied to his mother's apron strings, or anyone who cares that much for his mother could care no less for me. I chose to believe the latter and it was true." Bubba, a widow, lived with Libby and Richard for 29 years until she died at the age of 94. "Initially it was a huge adjustment for me, moving from a big city like Toronto where I had my family and friends to a small town. But when you want something to work, you make it work. You learn to make concessions." The bond deepened between Libby and her mother-in-law. "We adapted as the years went by because we both worked on our relationship," she said. "I could have easily thrown my hands up and said, 'I can't do this,' because her way of thinking and mine were worlds apart. But I learned a vital life lesson. You can get along with almost anyone if you want to make the effort." Libby's four children benefited from the arrangement as well. "Bubba was the matriarch and she was there for them. My children are better people because they lived in a home with an elderly person. They learned respect and what it means to be a family. They carry those same attitudes in their own lives." Richard and Libby enjoyed a wonderful close marriage of 43 years until he died in 1979. Libby is also blessed with nine grandchildren and seven great-grandchildren."

Shelley Stein would applaud Libby's ability to adapt to change. "So much depends on what your belief system and your perceptions are around transitional events in your life. At mid-life we need to be willing and able to view endings as beginnings; to view change as opportunity. For example, someone who retires can either feel positive—'I'm excited. I'll have time to travel'—or negative— 'I'm not productive any more, this is the end of my life.' Our

I eat in the dining room every night and use linen napkins.
Bertha, author

perceptions and beliefs determine how well we adapt. Our beliefs can change, and we want them to change to reflect our knowledge, experience, openness, and ability to embrace newness in life." Shelley then told me a story about a marriage in trouble as a result of a controlling, super-achiever who had to learn to adapt to being part of a couple. "My client, who had two alcoholic parents, learned early on that if she wanted anything done, she'd have to do it herself. As an eight-year-old she cooked her own meals, made her own lunches, and took care of the house. By the time she was 16, this A student had two part-time jobs. She had adapted to a style of 'cooking on all four burners' at the same time. Years go by. She becomes a lawyer and marries a lawyer. Their marriage is in trouble. Why? She must have control at all times. She has to have the last word on every decision and she doesn't trust her husband to follow through on commitments. The only other male she had had a close relationship with was her father, who disappointed her her entire life. She was shifting her fears, doubts, and expectations of negative outcomes from her father to her husband."

"So how did you help her?" I asked.

"I needed to teach her that what used to be adaptive was no longer effective. She worked on developing flexibility, to learn new ways of relating. One of the exercises I gave her was give-up-control day. For 24 hours, she was not allowed to make any decisions. She learned that her world didn't collapse as a result. Over time, as she progressed, her marriage improved significantly."

So there you have it. Two married women—one who meanders easily through life's ebbs and flows, and another who needs professional help to change her behaviour. Another psychotherapist friend, Carol Wise, gave me an interesting formula to remember the keys to change:

Awareness + Acceptance = Movement

She explained, "First you have to understand what the situation means to you, then you must accept it, find a place for it—a

I look forward to getting together with the same five or six guys every day for lunch—same place, same time—to talk about business, love problems and life in general.

Peter, construction manager

comfort zone—and then you need to change your behaviour. For example, let's say you are terrified of heights and you want to ski with your new boyfriend. The awareness may be that when you were a kid you fell out of a tree and you've never gotten over it. Acceptance is when you say, 'Okay, I know I'm afraid but I'm not going to stay stuck there. I am going to take care of myself with compassion and overcome this.' Movement—a change of behaviour—occurs when you go to the top of a ski hill and say, 'I am not that little girl any more, I am an adult. I can do this. I can ski down that hill and let go of the fear.'"

We must learn to renegotiate life with every challenge. Those who flourish have developed inner resources to adjust to changing circumstances. They demonstrate optimism and hope, high self-esteem, confidence, and resilience—no matter what happens—to cope with the stresses of life. Do not be afraid to shift, adjust, or alter your perception. Crisis and change are normal companions throughout life. Perhaps adapting for you means appreciating the good dishes that you inherited or the ones that came with your marriage. A happy, joyful life may depend on it.

LIFE IS NOT A SCREEN SAVER

There is a joke about a man given a choice by God to go to either Heaven or Hell. The man decided to check out Hell first and was astonished and delighted to see a beautiful, clean, sandy beach with clear water. There were thousands of beautiful women running around, playing in the water, laughing, and frolicking about. The sun was shining and the temperature was perfect. The man said to God, "If this is Hell, I really want to see Heaven!" God then showed him Heaven, which was a high place in the clouds with angels drifting about playing harps and singing. "Nice," the man thought, "but not a paradise like Hell!" He chose to go to Hell. Several weeks later, God went to see how he was doing and found

I go to church most Sundays.

Julie, nurse

him shackled in a dark cave among hot flames being tortured and burned by demons. The man cried out when he saw God, "This is not what I expected! What happened to the other place with the beach and the beautiful women playing in the water?" "Oh, that," God replied. "That was my screen saver!"

At our whim, we choose landscapes for our computer screen saver that convey peace, tranquility, and calmness. When we pause long enough, serene green forests, golden sunsets, or soothing ocean waves, often accompanied by glorious music, suddenly appear before our eyes. Ah, if only life were that predictable and perfect!

We must accept life just as it is, even with our own unchosen landscape of difficulties, pain, and loss. We run, we hide, we fight, we resist, and yet we must learn to live fully with the pain that life chooses for us. Acceptance doesn't mean we have to like what happens. No one welcomes adversity. But denying it or wishing it away is not the answer either. Psychiatrist Dr. Lawrence Ballon explains his approach. "My grief, my sadness, my problems are as much a part of my life as my vacation. We think that bad things shouldn't happen to us. When people fall ill and say, 'Why me?' I say, 'Why not you?' Who is it supposed to happen to? It happens to all of us. We must learn to accept the difficult times of our lives. People think that accepting what is means being passive. Acceptance is really embracing your situation realistically."

Helen Gougeon's philosophy echoes Dr. Ballon's words. Tethered to an oxygen tank to help her breathe, this optimistic 76-year-old journalist with pulmonary fibrosis has accepted her illness with grace. "It doesn't seem to be in my nature to feel sorry for myself or ask, 'Why me?' I'm alive. Every morning I wake up and say a grateful thank you. I have such a richness, a feeling of being blessed. I've accepted what has happened in my life."

I asked my boyfriend, Bernie, for his opinion. He replied, "I think asking, 'Why me?' is a legitimate question. It is human, in the face of loss, to go through a process of feeling sorry for yourself.

I get great pleasure from having a clean, tidy house.
                                                    Diane, photographer

How long you stay there is another matter." Bernie feels that "embracing one's situation realistically" sounds like giving up. "You must never give up hope. Try to change what it is possible to change."

Acceptance is a process—an evolution. You don't just wake up and accept a situation, but come to terms with your inability to change it over time—and then change your attitude instead. Bryant Kassirer, who suffered a stroke five years ago, has accepted that he has limitations. "There is a sense of loss in that I can't read or drive, and my memory has been affected. But I try to carry on as normally as I can. I've got no other choice but to accept what has happened. I couldn't have coped alone. Reesa has been there for me." Marital therapist Reesa Kassirer has now accepted her husband's ill health with a positive outlook, but it was painful getting there. "In the beginning, I was scared. I cried a lot, felt cheated and angry. I had to work through those feelings. You must meet what life hands you head on, and work through your pain to get to the good stuff. Bryant's stroke has totally changed our lives, but I now see the goodies we got from it. He is more open, giving, tender, and sensitive. Bryant always had these feelings inside, but I think coming to terms with his mortality was a catalyst. His illness brought us closer together. We can be together and feel totally fulfilled holding hands. The negative parts exist, but you take what is. What choice do you have?"

Accepting the loss of someone you love is the most difficult path that we must walk. We struggle with the finality, the reality of what has occurred. No loss is ever completely mourned. We are never finished with the process of acceptance. Even years after we have lost a loved one, like a broken glass that has shattered into millions of tiny fragments, a sliver can pierce us when we least expect it. Remembering their birthday, sharing a memory or celebrating a family tradition without them, or attending another funeral—all of these and more can open up our sadness as if the loss had just happened. During the busyness of our day we may

I grow bulbs in the winter and watch them bloom.

Steve, marketer

laugh and carry on with no hint of sorrow on our faces. But at night, in a darkened room, alone with our thoughts, tears may fall. Understand that these emotions will revisit us indefinitely. Acceptance involves peeling the sorrowful layers away to a deeper core of healing.

In 1972, Joseph Sorbara endured the devastating loss of his seven-year-old son. "I cried a lot," he recalled, with tears coming to his eyes. "I was angry. I didn't go for grief therapy but I wrote about whatever I was feeling—sometimes three lines or a page. I went to the cemetery a lot. I realized there was no point in asking why it had happened. There was no answer. Prayer and support from family and friends helped me. In my heart, the loss is always there. But time helps everything if you let it."

June Callwood admitted that she has not adapted to the loss of her son, Casey, who was killed at 20 by a drunk driver. "My son's death has left me a mess. I am not going to see him again. I have missed him every day of my life for the past 17 years, but I live with that."

At mid-life we are acutely aware of the ebb and flow of life—the beginnings and the inevitable endings yet to come. We may already know what it means to lose a grandparent, parent, spouse, child, friend, brother, or sister. Loss may come in the form of a divorce, a job or a role that defined us, even our lost dreams—the things that will never be. A physical illness or serious health change must also be grieved and accepted.

When psychologist Dr. Judy Turner counsels clients on adapting to loss, she speaks from experience. Her husband died when Judy was only 39. "People who have not suffered through loss don't realize why it takes the time that it does. We don't want to accept that there are situations in life that we can't control. We don't want to feel helpless. Our minds can accept only so much at a time. Acceptance is a very slow and gradual process." She then said something that instantly resonated for me. "When I have clients who feel loss so intensely that they have difficulty moving

In the morning, I look forward to enjoying a perfect grapefruit for breakfast.

Robert, consultant

on, usually they have not dealt with a loss they experienced at a much earlier age." It's true. When my marriage ended at 39, I sunk into a mass of quicksand. I couldn't seem to get myself unstuck, even with therapy, until I dealt with an earlier childhood loss. Judy says that clients sometimes feel guilty that they are adapting to their loss. "They worry that laughing and feeling better means that they are forgetting that person. What you want is to feel better. You are not being disloyal if you are happy again. 'If I really loved my husband, Joe, how could I enjoy someone else's company?' These thoughts can confuse people, but we need to allow that life does go on."

The best explanation of how healthy individuals deal with loss is found in the book *Life and How to Survive It* by John Cleese and Robin Skynner. "If a relationship has been happy and fulfilling, it can be easier to accept that you can't go on forever. The good memory of that sustains you. It's easier to let go of a relationship that has been good, because you don't feel guilty about it not working and you're not still trying to put it right. It is by mourning a loss that you recover from it. Self-pity is what you feel when you don't accept the loss." Robin's reaction, after losing his wife, shocked people who felt he should be suffering more than he was. "The sorrow I felt about losing her had a joyful quality in it when I remembered our good life together. If I had been more upset, wallowing in self-pity, people would have felt better. They could concentrate on feeling sorry for me instead of worrying about how they would cope with their own death or losing a partner."

A patient of mine, a young widow, mentioned to me that her friends asked her how she could experience happiness and feel joy just a year after she lost her husband. "I was basically a happy person before my loss, and certain aspects of the self don't change," she said. "One of my favourite quotes is 'Tragedy doesn't change who you are—it just shows you who you are.'"

So we know that life can still be joyful even after loss when we

Every night, I prop up the pillows, get into bed, and read for 15 minutes before going to sleep.

Daniel, marketer

are sustained with good memories. Jack Kornfield, an author, clinical psychologist, and Vispassana meditation teacher in private practice in northern California, has some thoughts on transforming the way we view our difficulties. "We must consciously take our unwanted sufferings, the sorrows of our life, the struggles within us and use them as a ground for nourishment of our patience and compassion, the place to develop greater freedom and our true Buddha nature. Difficulties are considered of such great value that a Tibetan prayer recited before each step of practice actually asks for them: *Grant that I may be given appropriate difficulties and suffering on this journey so that my heart may be truly awakened and my practice of liberation and universal compassion may be truly fulfilled.*"

It is almost counterintuitive to welcome this prayer into our lives, but think about its meaning: When we change our relationship to suffering by opening up our hearts to love and help others, miracles happen. To be open to life, even when loved ones die, requires a deep compassion for all human beings. Our pain often motivates us to want to help others. June Callwood created Casey House, a Toronto hospice to help those with AIDS, and named it for her son. She always has a place in her heart for Casey, but she still is able to enjoy life, finding joy and peace in everyday events. In a recent *Toronto Star* article she wrote, "In winters, Trent stays home now to write and play tennis. But the day after Christmas I drive to Fort Lauderdale and stay for a month. I pack my books, *New York Times*, sun lotions, split of wine, Trail Mix, fruit and beach chair every morning, then sit six hours by the sea watching people, and endlessly swimming. Then I'll make a small dinner, and read 'til I fall asleep. For me, like gliding, it's perfect peace."

Acceptance means we can't always change the outside world, but we *can* change how we see it. Dr. Lawrence Ballon gives a small but powerful example of how one man changed his attitude towards his office telephone. "A client who was a divorce lawyer was finding that answering his telephone was becoming an ordeal. The people calling him all day long were angry and unhappy;

I run six days a week for mental refreshment.

John, police officer

their lives were filled with problems. He had hypertension and heart disease from the stress. I taught him to do telephone meditation. When the phone would ring he would centre himself with a few breaths. He would let the phone ring two to three times and be clear in his mind that he was going to make this a meaningful and brief contact, neither becoming annoyed or pleased. He would try to deal with the phone in a state of equanimity, aware that there are people who are distressed. He dealt with them in a supportive way. The phone no longer became the enemy. It was just a tool that he was using in his work. He learned to control the state of mind that he brought to the telephone."

How liberating it must have been when this man accepted that the phone was just a phone, and not the root of his problem. And how often in life, when difficulty strikes, do we project our frustration onto others, as if it were our boss, our spouse, or our children who were the source of our problems. Just change them and we'll be happy. Rabbi Bernard Baskin comments, "Acceptance requires wisdom to know which situations we can change and which ones we can't, and God helps us to know the difference. We must meet each crisis, each adventure as it comes along. Equanimity comes with the understanding that we can't change everything."

In essence, our reluctance to accept change stems from our fear of change. Whether our courage to accept comes from faith or prayer, meditation, therapy, support from family and friends, or a deep personal conviction in the meaning of life, we must move forward. Remember that our computer screen saver depicting a Utopian world pops up only during inactivity. With movement, it disappears. In the same way, when we move towards acceptance, we understand that the real world is behind our screen saver. And we must live with it, just as it is. Using the good dishes, like life itself, comes with mixed blessings; the more fully we use them the greater the chance that they will chip, crack, or break. But, boy, did we have a good time while they lasted! Look at the experiences we shared and all the fun we had!

I take nature walks with my dog, Patrick, every day in High Park.
Carol, telecommunications analyst

BEING

Being

I'm so busy doing, haven't got time for being.
This frenzy of achieving is so self-defeating.
My mind is overloaded, the chatter is repeating.
Inside I should be looking, what am I not seeing?

I must create a space, a place where I can feel
That peace that comes with trust, in the me that's real.
It will happen in silence; I need to be alone.
Only then will answers come, and the truth I will own.

INNER SPACE

I wrote this poem several years ago as a reminder to myself to slow down after a particularly frantic time in my life. Instead of my normal routine of doing just two things at once, I was attempting to "squish eight more sardines into the can of life." Several friends who swear by meditation suggested that I might find the practice helpful. Well, I tried it and it has been a struggle for me. I just can't sit still in the morning and breathe in and out in a structured way. When I attempted to meditate before bed, I fell asleep.

Despite these early failures, I sensed that it might be good for me—sort of like eating kale. So every time I venture off to a spa or healing retreat where meditation is offered, I try it. Meditation seems to work better for me with a facilitator in a group setting (or maybe it's just being on vacation and away from everything!).

Last year, while I was on holiday at the Rancho La Puerta Spa in Baja, California, Deborah Szekely, the 77-year-old founder, used a simple yet powerful analogy to demonstrate our need for

Beckett, my golden retriever, comes to me with his favourite toy, an old sock, in his mouth, and we play tug-of-war.

Barbara, retired nurse

quiet reflection. She explained that if we have a cup filled right to the brim with tea and then add milk, the tea spills over into the saucer. Just like that cup, we all need room: a space to fill ourselves up, to daydream, think, reflect, grow, and gain insights. A space to meditate.

Psychotherapist Carol Wise agrees that we all need time to pause in our day. "In the old days, we were taught to type a period and then take two spaces before we began the next sentence. In the same way we must allow those two pauses in our day. Most of us want to put a comma or a semi-colon in our life and keep going on with our stuff. We need a period and two spaces for time to just be in the moment."

Roger Gabriel, a meditation teacher and the director of education for the Chopra Center for Wellbeing in California, learned to meditate in 1972 at age 24 when he worked in business as a management trainee. He quit his job after six months. "When I slipped into the silence, I realized that meditation was my future and that I wanted to teach others," he said. "This was my big awakening, but at the time I wasn't aware of it. It's often when we look back that we realize that a pivotal moment has occurred in our life." Roger took me into a meditation room at the Chopra Center and gave me a simple mantra (a phrase or word chanted over and over and aligned with breathing) to help me with my meditation practice. "Meditation just means awareness," he explained. "If you are walking and you're aware of walking then this is a walking meditation. The same thing occurs when you eat. While you read, watch TV, or have a conversation, most people remain unaware of their eating." Roger believes it is this general lack of awareness that prevents people from living more complete, joyful lives. "Think of life as a huge storeroom of treasures filled with everything we could possibly imagine. We walk through this room every day with a little flashlight because the room is pitch black. We shine the light on the floor because we don't want to trip over anything. All we see is what the light shines

I tap-dance twice a week.

Deanna, office manager

on. With meditation we learn to move the light around. We see things over here and there. If our senses are picking up all the celestial beings in this room but our belief system isn't strong enough to believe they exist, then we're actually filtering them out. Meditation allows us to see that it is all there and available to us."

Like Roger, Phyllis Pilgrim, a meditation teacher for 17 years at the Rancho La Puerta Spa, also found meditation so helpful that she wanted to help others find equanimity. A former geography teacher, she began yoga and meditation to get through a difficult marriage. "I got divorced, changed jobs and countries, and went halfway around the world to reflect on my life and look inward. Now, at 62, I embrace life without life owning me. I am in a central place where I can enjoy life fully from my own inner perspective." I asked Phyllis for a condensed version of Meditation 101. "We need to be quiet in order to hear our inner voice," she explained. "Only then will you be in touch with the you that's really you. Meditation puts you in a graceful place within your own life and gives you a sense of peace. Then when we are at peace we learn to let others be the way they need to be instead of wanting to control them." Phyllis summed up her thoughts: "Meditation allows you to be at peace with all the circumstances going on in your life, with the reality of life as it is."

In 1991, Bernie Klein's reality precipitated a complete lifestyle change that included meditation and visualization. After surviving a bout with cancer, he has found daily meditation practice sometimes difficult but always beneficial. "Some days my mind is too busy, but even if I feel it was not a good meditation, I know it helps me," he says. "Meditation gives me a sense of peace and quietens me down. It allows me to concentrate on one thing at a time. If I happen to miss a day, I am less focused and have more scattered thoughts."

In 1990, while doing some personal development training, Ellen Foster was introduced to the notion of beginning inner work and meditation practice, which she continued for eight

I read the comics every day in the newspaper.

Ellen, training manager

years. "I decided to join a Buddhist meditation group, thinking I would just learn to meditate," she said. "The surprise was that I got something I wasn't looking for—a spiritual path that made sense to me—and meditating 30 minutes a day is only one aspect of that philosophy." One year ago, however, Ellen went through a crisis, though she eventually confirmed that meditation was the right path for her. "I was facing some major decisions about leaving work, having a family, and starting my own business. I found that during this period of self-doubt and uncertainty my meditation practice was becoming work—something I had to do. I no longer had faith in the process." Ellen's Buddhist teacher suggested she stop the meditation exercises until she was ready to come back to them in a committed way. So after eight years of consistent practice Ellen stopped meditating for about nine months. "I learned a powerful lesson," she told me. "Changing my circumstances didn't make me happy. I quit my job. Did that help? No. Then I started my own business. Did that help? No. I dealt with fertility issues. Did that help? No. I came to the conclusion that all these major things did not contribute to my peace of mind. The only action that made a difference to my inner being was Buddhist insight meditation. My faith grew during this difficult time and I knew I had to return to meditation." Now Buddhism is again part of her life.

Lawrence LeShan, a psychotherapist and pioneer in exploring the therapeutic and ethical implications of meditation, would say that Ellen Foster had "come home." "When we meditate, we come home to parts of ourself that we had lost, to become fuller human beings, to gain serenity, peace, joy, greater efficiency in everyday life, to increase our power to love, to achieve a deeper view of reality, to more fully live the potential of being human," he writes in How to Meditate. "We meditate to find, recover, to come back to something of ourselves we once dimly and unknowingly had and have lost without knowing what it was or where or when we lost it."

My husband and I make a point of eating in the dining room with lit candles and music, five nights a week.

Kathi, showroom manager

PAYING ATTENTION

Philosopher and guru Dr. Deepak Chopra has inspired me for years. So when my boyfriend Bernie and I visited his Center for Wellbeing in La Jolla, California, I hoped, prayed—even meditated—that I might meet him, and perhaps even interview this prophet of alternative medicine for my book. What happened? He agreed to meet with me for five minutes! I was both nervous and excited. Perhaps his brilliance overwhelmed me. Using the same alphabet we all use, Chopra is able to articulate ideas and concepts of consciousness that are beyond most minds.

As I was escorted up the stairs into a reception area beside his office, my mind frantically considered several opening questions. Carol, his assistant, calmly advised me, "Detach yourself from the outcome. Just let it happen." Deepak came out of his office wearing grey sweats and running shoes. He shook my hand and I entered his private domain.

"I am really very busy," he began. "I don't have a lot of time."

I expressed my gratitude to him for seeing me.

"I don't know what I did with your book and poem. Tell me again, what are you doing?"

I tried not to show my disappointment. The day before I had handed him copies of *Passionate Longevity* and my poem "Use the Good Dishes." I expected that he had at least read my poem. Instead, he had no idea who I was or what I wanted. The clock was ticking so I quickly told him the name of my first book, and summarized the theme of this book, which I was working on at that time.

As I spoke, what I noticed more than anything were his eyes as they locked on mine. He was there—fully present, listening intently. I watched him watch me. He observed everything and missed nothing. There was no question that he was paying attention—as was I. I memorized every moment of the electrifying 300 seconds of my audience with this enlightened man. (To tap into his wisdom, see Chapter 8, Celebrating.)

I buy new bras and underwear.

Jackie, editor

We've all had the experience of someone not "being in the room" with us. Can you remember talking with someone at a cocktail party who was more interested in who else was there than in your conversation? Being in the room is part of a larger concept—being in the world. Many individuals sleepwalk through life. On automatic pilot, they only go through the motions of living. They may see everything as the big picture but focus on little. They drive home from work but fail to notice the fiery sunset reflecting brilliant gold off of office windows. Or they may eat dinner oblivious to the colour and tastes of the food and garnishes, or to the bouquet of spring flowers that adorns the table.

These small, ordinary, everyday moments keep our lives joyful and fresh. Life is then lived like an exclamation mark! To live fully each day we must pay attention and be mindful of everything. When you live this way, you anchor yourself in the present. This present-moment awareness is often called mindfulness. Derived from Zen Buddhism, it is a form of meditation in which you focus your attention on what you are experiencing from moment to moment. You don't think about what you are going to do next or what happened yesterday.

"See your life as a series of moments," suggests Dr. Lawrence Ballon, a psychiatrist who teaches meditation and mindfulness. "Most people have learned techniques to avoid coping with how they feel. They take a pill, overwork, overeat, overdrink—anything to change their state of mind. Picture someone listening to a pianist yet thinking about what happened at the office or whether they put enough money in the parking meter. That person is not fully present." He then cited an interesting example. "My dog lives in the moment. She's hungry; she eats. She's tired; she rests. She's aware of her own experience. She checks in with herself."

Psychiatrist Dr. Howard Book practises mindfulness and is acutely aware of his senses. "When I'm outside in the summertime, I can smell the earth and the green grass. In March I notice that the ground smells different. I smell the sweetness of spring coming.

I take a Sunday afternoon nap on the couch with the TV on.
Dennis, banker

Driving home from my office I am greeted by huge trees on both sides of my street, their canopy of leaves touching and kissing each other, dappled sunlight dancing among the branches. I see this every day and yet every day it thrills me. It's that kind of enthusiasm and paying attention that is important in my life."

Wendy Cecil-Cockwell has given her three children a gift by teaching them to notice the joy in small things. "Whether it's the sunrise, a snowfall, or the smell of toast, I point it out to them. Sometimes they laugh at me, but I believe that in every day there is something to celebrate. When I teach them to pay attention to small, ordinary things, it reinforces my belief. I am mindful of the seasons, of moments with a friend, of very small incidents that occur during the day that often slip by unnoticed."

Libby Dwor, 84, describes one of her favourite experiences, which involves her being present, mindful, and attentive. "Very often I go to the symphony by myself. I try to reserve the special choir seats that surround the back of the stage. I sit up there and watch the expressions on the conductor's face. I watch every musician. I am so involved in the music, I feel like I'm part of the orchestra."

I have been practising mindfulness for years, but never consciously labelled it. I've always loved to transform everyday experiences into extraordinary ones; to freeze-frame a moment so that time and thoughts stand still. Watching a cardinal in my backyard and listening to the repetitive chords of its song, witnessing a golden sunrise, or making love—these are magic moments when your life has meaning, when you feel connected to the universe or to another person. During the 15 years that I competed in marathons, I always ran fully engaged, focusing on my breathing, footsteps, and the timing of each mile. I was also keenly aware of my energy, my thirst, and my leg fatigue. I was fully present for each stride of those 26.2 miles.

We can learn to pay attention, to be more present and mindful of everyday life. Here is some advice from Dr. Ballon:

I "play wrestle" with my kids, age four and six, every night before bed so I can hear the best sound in the world: children's laughter.
                                                    Spencer, marketing consultant

- Start with just one experience, like taking a shower. Be in touch with your body, the sounds of the water, the smell of the soap, the sensations on your skin. Then move on to another experience.
- Eat an orange. Be mindful of the taste, the smells, the juice, the chewing and swallowing mechanism.
- When you are stopped at a red light, see this as an opportunity to take a full breath and relax.
- When working out at the gym, don't watch television or use a Walkman. Be with your breath and with whatever your body is experiencing. Pay attention to how your muscles feel.
- When having a massage, pay attention to each stroke and to your breathing.
- When you are outside, notice something pleasant each day, such as clouds, flowers, or leaves gently moving in the wind.

"Mindfulness," adds Dr. Ballon, "can also serve as a teacher or barometer of how effectively you are dealing with life's stresses or difficult people. When you pay close attention, you might notice, for example, that you are feeling fragile. Your next thought might be, 'My boss is really going to rattle my cage today.' On the other hand, if you are aware that you are feeling good, you might think, 'I can handle her today.' Mindfulness teaches you to notice what is going on and to handle stressful situations depending on how you feel. We must learn to embrace the difficult times—grief, sadness, problems—in our lives. All of us have attachments to the way we want things to be. Many people think, 'I should be happy or healthy,' or 'I shouldn't feel anxious.' Be with that anxiety. The more you fight the way you are, the worse it is. Mindfulness allows you to be with it all, just as it is."

After an inspiring week at the Chopra Center it was time to return to Toronto. Normally, on a long flight, I would dig into a pile of reading material and scarcely lift my head except to eat. Imbued with thoughts of Chopra and mindfulness, I decided to

Whenever I have insomnia, I send silent "love" messages to my friends' phone mailboxes.

Janet, dentist

take some time to revisit the whole experience. I glanced around at the other passengers. Across the aisle a little boy was sitting with his father. When the flight became a bit turbulent, his dad scooped him up, put the seat belt around both of them, and cuddled him, whispering soft, reassuring words. When the turbulence stopped, the child returned to his seat, sat there for a few minutes as if he were "checking in with himself," and then asked his dad to hold his hand. Dad's big hand reached over and the child held his thumb. I was so touched by this loving gesture: a small moment I would have missed if I hadn't been paying attention.

ONE HEARTBEAT AWAY

I will seize any opportunity to recite my favourite poem, "Use the Good Dishes." This is not an exaggeration. For example, since pilots can get rather bored listening to the incessant chatter of air traffic control, they often appreciate my sudden appearance and spontaneous performance inside the flight deck at 37,000 feet. (I just love a captive audience!) More recently, on a hiking holiday in southern Utah, I "entertained the troops" atop Snow Canyon Mountain with an open-air rendition. I'm not sure if God heard me, but two rattlesnakes nearby hissed their approval.

Why do I feel this urge to share my poem? Because every time I do, I hear inspiring stories. My poem triggers a dialogue. Other people's experiences spill out from the bottomless pitcher of Life. Everyone, it seems, has a "use the good dishes" story.

On my spa holiday, I heard this story from Martin Green, a Connecticut stockbroker for a large investment company. He learned a "life goes on" lesson while still in his early twenties. "I couldn't believe my eyes," he recalled. "I was sitting a few desks away when Don, the senior broker of the firm, suffered a coronary, slumped over, and died. Paramedics carried him out on a stretcher. Don's body wasn't even cold when Steve, the office

On my drive home each day, I make a point of calling my wife just to ask her if there is anything she needs or wants me to pick up.

Paul, bond trader

manager, started passing out choice names and telephone numbers from Don's prized client book. I'll never forget the expediency with which they dispersed the spoils. It was definitely business as usual."

"How did this experience change you?" I asked.

"I realized then and there that no one is indispensable and that you must enjoy life while you can. To those who are locked into work and whine to me, 'I can't take time off, they need me, I'm too busy,' I tell them, 'Life is so uncertain. You may not come home today.'"

Terri Licalzi, a spa pedicurist, understands Martin's philosophy only too well. One afternoon she lovingly attended to my feet, mangled from too many miles of hiking and running in the Utah wilderness. As she pumiced my calloused heels with rhythmic strokes, I recited my poem. Then she told me her story: "My brother drowned 15 years ago when I was 28," she recalled. "Brad was only 29 and the father of six kids. I remember the day after the accident. I stood there looking out the window, grief-stricken, crying, and numb while people walked past my house, laughing and having a good time. Kids were playing across the street; cars drove by as usual. I somehow thought that everything should stop because my brother was gone! I realized then that life does go on. This loss taught me to live fully each day. You never know when you will be next."

John W. thought *he* might be next. This financial analyst from New York sat beside me on the plane back from Utah. While most people in their thirties are busy making a living, for six months John was busy making deals with God to let him *live*. "I am 36 years old and gay," he told me. "My partner recently discovered that he is HIV positive. I felt terrible for him and worried sick for me. I had two choices. I could wait it out for an agonizing six months, which is the time it takes to see if the virus surfaces, or I could closely monitor my situation with a blood test every three weeks. There is a doctor in New York who processes blood tests in

Ever since I was 12 years old I have bought Vogue *magazine, and always eat a chocolate bar while I'm gazing at the pages of skinny models.*

Alma, physician

15 minutes for $80." John chose the latter.

How did he cope? "Every three weeks on 'blood test day' I woke up and said, 'Today is either going to be the best day ever, or my life as I know it will be over.' I made my way over to the doctor's office, had a blood test, and he'd say, 'Come back in 15 minutes.' I knew that in those 15 minutes my life could change forever. Then I wandered around Central Park, oblivious to everything and everyone around me—totally within myself and just talking to God. 'If you let me stay here...if you let me live...if you give me some more time here on earth...I will make a difference. I will serve you...I will repay you.'"

The blood tests continued to be negative after six months. John used to focus on his long-term goals and live for the future. Now he lives for today. "I realize that *living* today takes care of tomorrow. And I kept my bargain with God. I ran in the New York AIDS Run and raised $10,000 in pledges from everyone I knew. I have been doing weekly volunteer work at an AIDS hospice. I practise safe sex. I joined an organization that educates youth about AIDS. I have become a more compassionate, tolerant, loving human being. I see each day as a gift of life and I feel truly grateful."

I went to Utah to hike. I left those mountains with three poignant stories from Martin, Terri, and John, who were all jolted into realizing that life must be lived each day. This lesson is usually delayed until later in life. What I've come to understand through my relationships with older mentors is that all of us are only *one heartbeat* away from that great Hiking Trail in the Sky.

Helen Gougeon has learned this lesson. The vibrant retired journalist-broadcaster greeted me with a friendly smile and an oxygen tank. Pulmonary fibrosis, a lung disease, may have slowed her down, but she has a galloping spirit. "Because of my circumstances I can't run out the front door and walk to the grocery store as I used to. But I'm alive! Every morning I wake up and say a grateful thank you. Small pleasures mean so much to me. Last

I sit at the breakfast table nursing my first coffee of the day.
                                                    Dave, business manager

Saturday, the daughter of my oldest and dearest friend took me out to do some errands. I bought birthday and Valentine cards, mailed a few letters, bought some flowers. Then we went to Starbucks and had a coffee and chatted. I've known her since she was nine. I came home and I was as happy as if I had seen a play on Broadway!"

My aunt Libby Dwor loved life even before her near-fatal car accident ten years ago. Now, at 84, her unbridled joy for each day is palpable. "It was a terrible head-on collision. The drunk driver who hit me was killed and I almost died. I had so many broken bones that doctors said if I lived I'd never walk again. After four months in the hospital I walked out. I don't treat life lightly. It is such a wonderful gift to be alive!"

My aunt Gert Kushin, 82, is severely limited by osteoporosis and Parkinson's disease, yet feels truly blessed to be alive. "It may take me an hour to get out of bed, but that's beside the point. I am so thankful even though I am tied to a walker, bent over with back pain. I'm here. I can talk to my family and friends; go out for a cup of coffee. That's so important to me. Time doesn't mean anything to me because I'm not rushing anywhere. I don't worry about how long things take me as long as I get there. When I wake up and realize I'm alive, I say thank you to God for giving me another day. I live every moment of each day."

CARPE DIEM

When I first mentioned to people the subtitle of this book, *Finding Joy in Everyday Life*, I was charmed to hear in response about the small pleasures that especially touch family, friends, and patients. I understand from my own life how the most simple, ordinary things can give meaning and purpose to my day, allowing me to connect to the present. I can be motionless with delight while watching a blue jay on a tree branch. The world can stop as I

Every week I get lost for hours in my favourite bookstore.
Susan, teacher

inhale the smell of fall leaves or feel the warmth of the sun on my face. My mind is empty of thoughts as I sit in front of a crackling fire, listening to music unfold its symphony of sounds.

Hoping to record their responses for this book, I began to ask everyone I came in contact with, "How do you find joy in everyday life?" The contributions, printed on the bottom of each page of this book, are inspiring for us all. I realized more than ever that we don't need much to make us happy. If we wait for the big things in life to do that, such as meeting the right person or achieving financial security, we'll miss the little gems that occur every day. In the overall scheme of things, each magic moment is like a heartbeat: Just as one heartbeat multiplied millions of times creates the continuous flow of life, these small joys multiply to give continuous life to our days.

Contemplate each of these small pleasures: eating a perfect grapefruit, running through the park, paddling a canoe, listening to loons on a lake, a new flower that unexpectedly blossoms in your garden, chatting with your grandchildren, walking your dog, cuddling with your children, a hot bubble bath on a rainy day, freshly squeezed orange juice, the freshness of a new morning, the smell of your morning coffee, warm water tingling on your back in the shower, hummingbirds suspended above a bird feeder, a wonderful massage. These are only a handful of the answers I received from those who take *carpe diem* (seize the day) to heart.

Recently, I had a wonderful chat with flight attendant Carol Hayes about an activity that has given her such joy that she tingled with excitement just describing it. "Once a week I take my golden retriever, Reiker, to Ste. Anne's Hospital in Quebec to do pet therapy with the patients. Reiker carries a stuffed teddy bear in his mouth and wriggles with joy as we make our way to each bed. I love to watch each patient's smiling face as they pat my dog on the head." She could hardly contain herself as she told me of a surprise she was planning for Halloween. "Reiker is visiting the hospital dressed up as a fire chief with a red hat, a little yellow

I relish those 15 minutes alone driving to work, sipping a frappacino, listening to classical music.

Jeannie, salesperson and mother of three

jacket, and an axe on the side. The hat has FIRE CHIEF print-ed on it." She giggled. "I can hardly wait to see their faces. To me, this simple pleasure is better than winning a million dollars in the lottery."

Writer-director Reva Stern undergoes joy therapy every day at noon, and doesn't even have to leave her second-floor condo-minium to experience it. "My window faces a courtyard attached to a high school for performing arts," she told me. "Every day I rush to the open window at lunch hour to listen and watch kids rehearse and interact with each other. They might practise acro-batics or fencing, or exchange ideas on how a scene might be played. They are so full of talent, hope, and promise that each day when I hear them laughing together, I am reassured that the world is okay."

Breakfast in bed may be a fantasy for some, but for June Callwood, 75, it's a daily joy thanks to her husband, Trent Frayne. "This ritual began 36 years ago when I was experiencing terrible morning sickness with my fourth pregnancy," she said. "Trent began bringing me dry toast and a little bit of tea in bed, then he would give the kids breakfast and see them off to school. This went on for months. By the time my stomach was steadier he was used to making me breakfast, and he liked doing it. What began as a temporary measure has continued to this day." What's on the menu? "Trent brings me fruit, toast, herbal tea, plus two newspa-pers, which I love to read in bed."

Artist Doris McCarthy, 89, doesn't look for big things to make her happy. "A wonderful slice of toasted homemade bread covered with marmalade, a juicy sweet Florida orange—these are small, wonderful treats I appreciate each day. You know you're happy when you're aware of the small pleasures that every day offers you."

I am reminded of something that the late Gary Lautens wrote in his weekly column for the *Toronto Star*: "Send the flowers while *you* can still smell them." In other words, don't postpone joy. It is

---

I give my sleepy 11-year-old dog a pat on the head as I'm leaving for work at 5:15 a.m. He always acknowledges it with a half-hearted lift of his tail.

Neil, banker

there for you in small ways every single day. A smile, a hug, a kind word, a flower, a book, or a song may make all the difference. All you have to do is open your eyes and seize the moment.

THE BIRDS AND THE TREES

No matter how many times I witness the unfolding of spring, I am always giddy with excitement. Last year, Nature decided to play a symphony of surprises for me at the country inn where I was staying for the weekend. I stared with childlike wonder at a nest perched on top of a 20-foot-tall white pillar that supports the patio's cedar and glass overhang. In full view, Mother Robin sat watchfully, intermittently nuzzling her three babies with her beak. I was in love with this magic moment. It was raining, and the rhythm section of Nature's orchestra drummed a soft pitter-patter on the glass roof. My senses were flooded as I inhaled the smell of wet grass. I heard the distant cawing of crows and the tin-like call of a toad beckoning me to the nearby pond. I walked over, curious about the water and its banks. Pale blue hummingbirds suspended like helicopters sampled nectar from bright yellow irises. Tall, green reed grasses gently undulated in the rain. Water lilies reached out to the borders of the pond. It was mating season for the toads, and as I looked below the surface of the water I saw thousands of black tadpoles darting like torpedoes about the dark green algae. Occasionally my footsteps disturbed a toad who hopped safely into the water. Beyond the pond I noticed a forest with tall, symmetrical Scotch pines in the front and French lilac and bridal veil spirea at the base of their trunks. A large catalpa tree was not yet in bloom. Finally the rain stopped and my eyes focused on a grey dove perched on a lush branch of a camperdown elm. The crows were cawing louder, piercing the air with a steady shrillness. I returned to the patio to watch the robins. Father Robin had taken over and was feeding worms to the three greedy

I do the cryptic crossword in the newspaper every day.
                                                              Stephen, analyst

open mouths. This was the wonder of early morning on a damp spring day in the country.

Everything I know about life I learned from Mother Nature. I had to be motionless for the true understanding to come. Only in our be-ing, our sitting, paying attention, and listening will we see Nature spring into action. Who knows what fresh insights may accompany a breath of sweet lilac perfume wafting through the air. While you quietly contemplate the clouds, an overwhelming sense of connectedness to the universe may envelop your soul. I've learned patience from tiny delicate green shoots that refuse to be coaxed into growing faster. The giant catalpa tree in my garden also takes its time; it's always the last one to show off its leaves at Nature's surprise party. Nature teaches us about the ageless and timeless cycle of rest and renewal, of rebirth and death, of cruelty and beauty coursing through the earth, forests, mountains, and streams. I rejoice with the predictable return of my hosta plants, their tentacles spreading farther with each season. I was upset by the destruction of my magnolia tree one fierce winter, when ice-laden skeletal branches lay fractured and strewn about my front lawn, and I learned about adaptability for my own life. Like trees, we may be tossed and blown by the ravages of life, but stay steadfastly rooted and resilient in the aftermath. There is a continuity to Nature. As I am blessed to wake up on each new day, I am grateful for the regularity of morning spreading rays of light across the sky. I relish the simplicity and mystery of Nature. How do ants know where to find my pink peony bushes each spring? And why do ants and not bees stimulate the growth of the blossoms? I am delirious with excitement as I witness a surprise rainbow, or a big yellow full moon, or the first winter snowfall blanketing the earth. With the wonder and awe of a child, I find what I long for through Nature: beauty, stillness, strength, and peace.

I take off my suit and tie when I come home and change into jeans.
Michael, pension fund manager

HUSH

At the corner of 72nd St. and Madison Avenue in Manhattan, my girlfriend Linda suddenly voiced what I had been thinking. "Just listen to the noise." Wailing sirens, cars and trucks honking in city gridlock, jackhammers pummelling the pavement, and the roar of an airplane assaulted our ears. After three days of being in the city that never sleeps, my head felt scrambled. Fatigued and irritable, I was eager to escape to the quiet of my Walden Pond in Toronto.

Noise is so much a part of the landscape of everyday life that most of us aren't aware of the physical and emotional erosion it causes. Studies have found that chronic noise is a health hazard that, over time, increases stress levels. The body and mind crave stillness, quiet, solitude. Sometimes we are astonished by a quiet, beautiful moment in our life. Paddling a canoe on a lake, walking through a forest, or standing in a gentle snowfall at night are examples of awe-inspiring tranquil moments. Years ago, while camping on a remote island up north, I was shocked when I realized that I could hear the flapping of a bird's wings overhead. Another time, during a power failure in the neighbourhood, I was amazed at how quiet a house really is without the humming of electrical appliances.

I am convinced that quiet time, a regular daily retreat from the noise and routines of everyday life, is necessary for a joyful life. Dr. Herbert Benson, author of *The Relaxation Response* and associate professor of medicine at Harvard Medical School, has studied the physiological and emotional effects of relaxation for more than 20 years. The first step towards achieving what he calls the relaxation response is finding a quiet environment. "One must turn off not only external stimuli but also external distractions. I consider quiet to be unoccupied, uninterrupted time."

Joseph Sorbara finds solitude in the underground garage of the office building where he runs a family business. For almost

I take out the cedar strip canoe on early summer mornings at the cottage and paddle on a silent, still lake.

Sandy, professor

two years he's been "hiding out" inside a private storage room equipped with only a carpet, desk, and chair. "I try to get an hour to myself to read, smoke a cigar (there's an exhaust fan), jot down a few notes, or put my feet up and just think." he says. "No one can reach me unless I turn on my cellphone. And no one can find me. It's wonderful! If for some reason I'm unable to set aside that quiet time during the day, I notice I'm not as patient at home. That hour of solitude allows me to be present with my wife and children."

Therapist-mediator Resa Eisen is trained to tune in to the feelings of clients, and she also knows when she needs to listen to her own gut. "Every day I take a pause for about 30 minutes," she explains. "I need to take myself out of my environment. I might go for a walk, or close the door, ignore the phone, even nap for 20 minutes. There's no agenda, it just *is*. Something clicks inside of me and I just know when it's time to be quiet."

For many of us, quiet time occurs only when we finally turn out the lights and collapse in bed. However, that is often when those infinite to-do lists start marching out of the walls and into our minds. We don't need much solitude to renew—even 15 minutes out of your daily schedule free from interruptions is restorative. Dr. Pam Letts, a busy Florida physician, has discovered one painless way to find quiet time. "I used to listen to music and tapes while driving my convertible to work," she explained. "Now I enjoy the silence during that 30-minute commute. I get lost in my own thoughts. I notice things, like the sun reflected on windows of office buildings. I just love the stretch of water on either side of the causeway. At night, going home, I feel the wind on my face and can see the stars. I return home in peace."

My patients would be surprised at how quiet my home is. I take my high-energy, chatty personality home each day and open the door to cherished calm. While I regularly listen to music in my car, there is no music or television on at home except for the nightly news while I'm getting ready for bed. In the summer, I

Every morning I check in with the outside world by looking up at the sky and seeing what the weather is like.

Brian, administrator

am lulled to sleep by the sounds of crickets, a familiar sound from childhood, when I lived out in the country. Now that I am cat-less, there isn't even a meow breaking the silence!

For those who don't live alone, quiet time does not have to mean total silence. Sitting still in front of a crackling fire, listening to raindrops as they hit a window, even a tape of ocean sounds can be healing and renewing. I know a couple who have a unique method of communicating their need for solitude to each other. When he wears a beloved baseball cap or she wears a favourite sweater, it sends the message: "Don't talk to me right now. I need to be quiet with my thoughts."

Then there is the method that one of my patients uses to find an oasis in life. While the world is sleeping, 80-year-old Henry Den Braber finds solace running a ten-kilometre route through silent city streets in Toronto. "In the summer I wake up at 4 a.m., do 20 minutes of stretching, and I'm usually out the door by 4:30. The streets are deserted, except for the occasional newspaper delivery person. I love to hear the birds announcing the first light of day. This is my quiet time to think and be alone: just me, my heartbeat, and the rhythmic sound of my footsteps!"

IT'S ABOUT TIME

TWO SECONDS! Just last week, a reckless motorist sped through a red light, hoping to save two minuscule seconds. One irresponsible moment cost him his life and injured two children, who are now recovering in the hospital.

Why does it seem as if the world today is permanently stuck on fast-forward? Watch the groceries some people buy, washed, bite-sized lettuce in a bag, or carrots, peeled and bagged to save time. Bottled "homemade" soup and prepared foods are flying off the shelf. Do you find yourself doing two or three things at one time, such as eating lunch and writing a memo while talking on the

I look into the smiling eyes of my three children every day.
Jennifer, human resources

phone? Computers have created a sense that the world should move quickly. Wait ten minutes and a faster version will emerge. If your idea of a perfect day is being on the right side of advance green lights at intersections, or your life is one big drive-through, maybe it's time to slow down and push life's pause button.

I can think of at least 100 occasions when I have rushed frantically to get somewhere—the airport, a dental appointment, a publisher's meeting, the hairdresser—only to be told to wait when I arrived breathless and damp under the arm. So what was the point of all that sprinting anyway? How can I free myself to take my time?

I drove to a dreaded intersection near my house, a notorious corner with the slowest traffic lights in the city. You know, the kind where every lane of cars moves in turn except yours—and you're always the last? Usually I sit there and curse, "There goes five whole minutes!" This time, working on being mindful, I actually timed the wait with a stopwatch. To my surprise, it was only 75 seconds! My perception of time is starting to change.

You will read my theory about the origins of this "hurry" syndrome in Chapter 5, Playing. We all know that kids are in a huge rush to grow up. Whatever adults have, they want, and the sooner the better. The minute they are old enough they are out getting their beginner driver's permit. One of the first "grown-up" items that kids want is a watch. I believe this item is a symbol of the beginning of the end of childhood. Think of the meaning of the word "watch." It is a homograph (a word identical in spelling with another but different in meaning). We watch a watch, which keeps us focused on time. Spontaneity and playfulness are reduced and often replaced with a more rigid notion of what we should be doing. Recently, Bernie and I went to the movies with another couple. Although the three-hour movie we planned to see had received outstanding reviews, the other couple were concerned that it was too long. The "endurance" aspect never entered my mind. I was focused instead on what a thrill it was that someone

I treat myself to raspberries and blackberries in the winter, when they're expensive.

Joyce, *bartender*

had created a masterpiece so entertaining and engrossing that it would provide me with that much enjoyment. (I visited the ladies' room before the movie began!)

I have always been fascinated by the perception of time. A five-hour flight can seem much shorter when a good conversation is added to it. When someone says, "I'll call you right back!" even a ten-minute wait for the return phone call seems long. And why, now that I'm over 50, do the weeks seem to fly by? A friend, Michael Levy, described it perfectly when he said, "I woke up Monday morning and discovered it was Friday night!"

Here's a riddle: When does a week seem like only a day? For the answer, take a second to read my poem.

For the Time Being

When you're 15, wanna be 16, 12 months is hardly near.
Grieving over a loss? Why it's only been a year!
A month just drags on, with crutches and a cast,
But given a month to live? A second goes too fast!
The meeting is postponed. Another week of frustration!
Is it Friday already? Damn this short vacation!
One more day 'til I see him, my heart can hardly wait,
The doctor wants to see me, tomorrow I'll know my fate.
A 60-minute plane ride, an hour too long if it's rough.
A relaxing one-hour massage—it's never long enough!
Another red light to stop me, 60 seconds, then I blast!
A goodbye-I'll-see-you-soon kiss, please let this minute last.
Time imprisons or it frees you,
It depends on your perception.
After you read this, *please take time*,
to pause for some reflection.

Every morning I take my coffee, sit on the dock, and look out at the lake.

George, plant manager

MUSIC: SOUND HEALING

Whenever I hear the Enrique Iglesias song "Bailamos" on my car radio, I turn up the volume and bounce on my seat to the beat of the salsa rhythm. Finally I bought the CD so I could listen to it any time. One afternoon while taking a break from writing, I danced shamelessly in my living room. What joy! I love music. A song can trigger a twinge of remembrance, a zing of romantic love, or just pure bliss. Music keeps me riveted to the present.

Musical rhythm, melody, and harmony also stimulate several areas of the brain, reducing anxiety and depression and lowering blood pressure and heart rate. Rhythm has a powerful organizing effect on motor skills. Stroke victims walk more steadily upon hearing a piece of music with a strong, even rhythm. Some hospitals prescribe music before cardiac surgery and during chemotherapy. Jon Kabat-Zinn, Ph.D., director of the stress-reduction and relaxation department at the University of Massachusetts Medical Center, suggests to patients that they listen to a tape on mindfulness meditation accompanied by harp music prior to surgery. "I felt the meditation instructions would be more accessible to the patients within the flow established by the music. The harp has traditionally been an instrument used for healing and calming the mind."

Music sounds the way emotions feel, believes Kye (Carol) Marshall, a psychotherapist who is also a cellist and composer. She uses music when she wants to reach beyond or underneath words in a session with a client. "Music as a form of communication can access our inner world, particularly our emotions and feelings, reaching those non-verbal, repressed, and defended areas of our psyches," she says. In her office she has a vast array of instruments that are easy to play. The client chooses an instrument and plays a theme—a feeling, sensation, person, or image—that has come up verbally. Kye will then improvise on the piano, cello, or any of the other instruments, focusing on attuning musically

I wear fabulous lingerie every day—sexy brassieres and lacy thongs.
                                             Jeanne, TV personality

with the client. "I always tape our music-making," she says. "When we finish playing, I have the client relate verbally how he or she found the experience."

Phil Nimmons, 76, composer, clarinetist, recording artist, and Officer of the Order of Canada, feels that music is both biologically and artistically a part of the human experience. "My life fills me with music. It's around us all the time—birds, the sounds of nature. Music is an expression of our feelings. I can't imagine life without it. I am in the moment when I play my clarinet every day."

Music and song gives expression to something that may be difficult to express any other way. I remember crying out all the pain of a failed marriage during the therapeutic singing sessions at Esalen, a healing retreat in Big Sur, California. Explains psychotherapist Carol Wise, "When we sing, we use the body—the very essence of our being—as an instrument. When we talk, we control our words and thoughts. But we let that go when we sing. We let go of the fear and let our inner voice out." Carol loves music and listens to Gregorian chants when she wants to be calm, peaceful, and present. "The music helps me get in touch with my feelings, " she says. "The sounds connect to my soul. It embraces me—just like taking a warm, soothing bath."

After reading a copy of my poem "Use the Good Dishes," singer Michael Burgess commented: "Life becomes more satisfying on all levels if one can only master the art of living in the moment, of using the good dishes to set all the tables of one's life. I think it takes passion, commitment, a lot of laughter—and lots of broken dishes!" Whenever I hear him sing I am truly living in the moment, with tears in my eyes; the sound of his powerful voice stirs emotion and hope within my heart. In a recent *Toronto Star* article, Burgess described the concerts at Princess Margaret Hospital, where he performs for cancer patients, as one of the great experiences of his life. "There is so much emotion. It can be hard to keep your voice going. But I have gained even more respect for the impact of music. I really believe that music can

I take a spoon and a litre of heavenly hash ice cream and polish it off.
Jack, ad executive

help healing. You must not underestimate the power of hope."

Don Wright has been singing his whole life. This 91-year-old musician, arranger, composer, conductor, and educator carries a tune in his brain synchronized to his footsteps during his 45-minute daily walk in the neighbourhood. "I sing to myself and walk to the beat of 6–8 music. Life has a rhythm, and music is rhythm." When Lillian, his musical partner and beloved wife of 57 years, was in failing health, Don would go upstairs to the bedroom with his ukulele and they'd sing together. "She sang with me the night before she died. Music was the bond we shared together."

One of my life mentors, Deborah Szekely, 77, believes that music teaches us about living life as a process. "When you put a needle on a record you're there to listen to the music, not to get to the end of the record." As the musical notes unfold, we are anchored in the present.

AND HOW WAS <u>YOUR</u> DAY?

Imagine you're on the subway going home from the office. At least a hundred people are in the car with you, reading, dozing off, whispering, standing, and swaying to the rhythm. One hundred human beings at one particular moment of time are sharing the same physical experience in the same place on Earth. It's funny about closed spaces like elevators and subway cars: People are naturally reticent around strangers. But suppose that for one moment each person travelling with you on the subway was willing to tell you one significant thing that had happened to them that day. What stories would you hear? If we are all on a journey, what would we discover by stepping into a chapter of someone else's life?

Today...Someone realized that he is in love, quit smoking, experienced her first kiss, lost a pet, began an affair, resolved a family rift, shaved for the first time, found money on the street,

Every morning I kiss and hug my wife.

Mory, retired entrepreneur

rekindled a friendship, cried over the loss of a loved one, bought her first home, made a will, told his parents he was gay, said "The cheque is in the mail," felt lonely in a relationship, had a birthday, broke a heart, started his first job, repeated the same mistake, told a white lie, found that missing sock, broke a promise to a child, filed for divorce, made another excuse not to exercise, thought money would solve every problem, discovered a lump in her breast, found his first grey hair, slept in and was late for work, became a grandparent, said "He's in a meeting," told a secret, reached a goal, went on another diet, cheated the government, missed her period, moved in with a lover, said "I'll call you" and did, decided to quit his job, began psychotherapy, dreamed of winning the lottery, was in the right place at the right time, became a senior citizen, paid off a debt, made a child feel loved, wasted the day.

The next time someone asks, "How was your day?" resist the temptation to give a routine answer like "Okay, I guess," or "Fine," or "Not bad," or "Can't complain." Instead, think about this simple truth: Today you have traded one day of your life in return for the experience of joy, struggle, victory, loss. So, *how was your day?*

I exchange e-mails with my son who lives in Israel.

Dina, office manager

UNBURDENING

Stuffed

When you're stuffed with enough, too possessed
by your possessions,
When you shudder at the clutter, and
your places have no spaces,
When acquiring's not inspiring, getting more is but a bore,
Then it's time to say goodbye. Hear my cry. Simplify!

A strange thing has been happening since I turned 50. I've put my house on a diet, shedding excess baggage in the form of furniture, tchotchkes, even cats—live and ornamental. I liposuctioned over forty pounds of clothing into six large green garbage bags. The process of throwing stuff out is liberating for my body, soul, and closets. Call me energized, cleansed, moulted; just don't call me to ask whether I want your stuff!

I confess I had help with my "diet" from the queen of de-clutter, Liz Manore. A professional home and office organizer, her "less is more" philosophy motivates companies and individuals to take stock of their stock and junk all their junk. Like a detective she walked from room to room carefully investigating the evidence spilling out of crowded cupboards and closets. The transformation took six hours. Now my suits, skirts, blouses, and pants are all neatly arranged according to season. Like an old romance, the unloved clothing was discarded (with ruthless Liz standing over me) and given to charity.

Once I began the process of simplifying my life, it was easy to move on to the next challenge—the annual street garage sale. Every year bargain hunters and dealers descend like vultures on my street, picking through my junk (which they think is good stuff). Then they sell it to someone else in their annual garage sale! In

Every day I go outside and look at my garden to see what has bloomed.

Witold, massage therapist

one of his famous routines comedian George Carlin joked, "A house is just a pile of stuff with a cover on it." Why do we accumulate so much? According to Liz, "Most people never have a regular cleanout event. That, coupled with our consumer-oriented need to buy more, newer and better stuff, means we keep acquiring until our physical space just can't hold any more." If we let it, life could become one giant garage sale full of junk. Now that I am a convert, I know that clutter is an energy drain. Think of the time it takes just to find things, not to mention the effort expended deciding where to put everything.

My family is thrilled with the reduced version of my home, especially when they are the recipients of my "good junk." At my brother's home, you'll find limited-edition prints (leftovers from my "ex"-files), a top-of-the-line cappuccino machine that I had every intention of using but didn't, and a large fitness unit complete with dust (I joined a club). I feel joyful knowing that I am helping them. I can't wait to unload something good and useful on my two newly married nephews.

Now if the animal lovers who are reading this promise not to picket my house, I will reveal a difficult decision I've made to reduce my stress level. I am known by family and friends as a cat lover. For the past 20 years, Wellington and Napoleon were my "children in fur coats." They were Humane Society kittens who grew into loving, well-behaved companions. Since they both read my first book, they enjoyed passionate longevity of 19 and 20 years, respectively. After they died, I began to enjoy my fur-free sabbatical. My freedom was short-lived. I couldn't resist adopting two-year-old pedigreed Himalayan sisters desperate for a good home. My first mistake was naming these prima donnas Coco and Chanel. They became high-maintenance "designer cats" who did everything but borrow my gold card and shop at Holt Renfrew. Although they were very cute and loving, they both resented every minute I worked or travelled and was unavailable to tend to their every whim. Cats have a clear way of communicating their

Every night my sweetie and I have a ritual: hug-hug, chat-chat, read-read, then we go to sleep.

Rifka, bookkeeper

displeasure. My home was becoming a giant litter box. Do you know what it's like to return home from a wonderful day at the office only to open the front door to a foul mood and a foul smell? The real issue was my absence. My diagnosis: (Not-Enough) Attention-Deficit Disorder. So after two years of investing in plug-in room deodorizers, air fresheners and carpet powder and cleaners, I gave my cats to Michael, a close friend who works out of his home. I am happy to report that all is well. Both cats are content and using the litter box as prescribed.

Most of the older adults I interviewed for this book spoke of unburdening as a welcome process. As their life evolved, they found meaning in relationships and activities, not in things. Attachments were forged in friendships and family, not in acquisitions. As Doris McCarthy, 89, says, "As we age, we find out how many things we once wanted that we just don't need any more." For many, moving to more compact surroundings is a joyful opportunity to furnish the homes of children and grandchildren. But Libby Dwor would not agree with Doris. An elegant, remarkable woman who has given her life to family, philanthropy, and community, she is planning to move into a fabulous, new, roomy condominium in the heart of Toronto. Many of her friends have downsized into small retirement residences, but not her. "I don't believe in diminishing my living. Every time you get rid of something you make your life smaller."

One afternoon, my hairdresser, Robert Gage, aptly summed up the three stages of life: "In the early parts of life you acquire things, in the middle portion you have things, and in the last part of your life you edit or get rid of things." Even Barbra Streisand is unburdening these days! At 57, preferring the simpler beach life of scrubbed pine and seashells to Hollywood, she is selling all her cars, shoes, pianos, handbags, art, and antiques. (She's keeping James Brolin, though!) She says she has "evolved into a more relaxed style of life" where worldly goods are less important. I mean, just how many $1000 handbags does a girl need, anyway?

I have a big bowl of porridge with brown sugar, milk, and bee pollen.
Norm, retired educator

When I asked Rabbi Bernard Baskin, 80, his opinion on simplifying our lives, he reminded me that when Gandhi died, everything he owned fit into a shoebox. He also quoted Plato, who once remarked while strolling through a marketplace, "Look at all the things I can do without!"

My mother hated clutter. She was always throwing things out without consulting any of us. My brother Steven and I wish we still had our Howdy Doody doll, and I'd love to get my hands on some of the antiques she sold for a song. But thankfully, she never threw out photographs or personal mementoes, so I cherish my carton filled with public school report cards, drama awards, snippets of my first curls, and a letter I wrote from camp when I was a very homesick eight-year-old.

What would make your life simpler, slower, and more joyful? Do you suffer from piles? Piles of outdated magazines, newspapers, and books? A friend of mine too busy to cook refuses to throw out her 20-year-old (and growing) collection of gourmet food magazines on the off chance that she may need a recipe someday. What things are you holding onto that create stress in your life?

NOT GUILTY!

"Anybody over 60 with an ounce of foresight can start to see the light at the end of the tunnel," Judge Hugh Locke, 72, said with certainty. "By the time you are 70, the light is getting a lot closer. Even when you are 50, you can see a small pinprick of light. Naturally, your time becomes precious and you become selective about the people with whom you want to enjoy your life."

In the last year I've been acutely aware of the passage of time and that nasty pinprick of light. Book deadlines and speaking engagements a year away have an imperceptible way of pulling me fast-forward into the future. When you find yourself praying for

I want each passenger in my cab to feel it was a good experience, so I'm friendly and I listen to traffic reports for the best route.
Barry, taxi driver

voice mail because a "live" person takes too much time, learning to say no is a necessity. No is a choice. I *choose* what's important to me and how I want to spend my time. This sounds good in theory, but in reality I am an extrovert, so I sometimes overload myself with social engagements. Then comes the inevitable wrestling match between my head and my heart. Why did I agree to go? Should I cancel? If I don't go, they'll be upset and I'll feel guilty. Because my life seems full of opportunities, the challenge for me is to stay focused and make choices that align with my goals. However, just when I feel I'm in control, the phone rings and someone offers me something I can't resist.

As a chiropractor, I palpate the ravages of stress. For those patients aged roughly between 30 and 49 who race into my office, cellphone in hand, I am just another appointment they must fit into their busy schedules. While I am manipulating their joints, they tell tales of trying to juggle careers, kids, spouses, parents, and social activities in a never-ending push-pull scenario. Too many choices, a dose of guilt, and lack of sleep, compounded by an intense personality, wears them down over time. Flu or severe back pain, the body's homeostatic system communicating its anger, forces them to slow down. Here is one example of how guilt can cause illness. A patient limped into my office with acute pain at the back of her right thigh. Her physician had diagnosed her condition as a pinched nerve and she had left with the usual prescriptions for pain. When she swore to me that she couldn't recall twisting, lifting, or falling, I decided to probe deeper into her story. She revealed that for several weeks she had been away from home working out west on a special project for her company. Her beloved, aging dog became very ill soon after her departure. Unable to be with him, she received nightly updates in phone calls to her husband. In between sobs, she told me that her dog had been diagnosed with a lymphoma in his right back leg and had been put down. "I never said goodbye to him," she cried. "He was a puppy when I got him and became my best friend." I suggested

Every day I try to help a friend.

Andrea, real estate agent

that she had taken on her dog's suffering out of guilt. The location of their pain was identical—this was not coincidental. "Along with my therapy," I directed, "I want you to write a letter to your dog asking for forgiveness. Tell him how much you loved him and what a difference he made in your life." She did. Within a week, the pain was gone.

For many of us, turning 50 represents a growing awareness of our need for physical, emotional, and spiritual well-being. In the strainer of life we have sifted out the lumps that clog up our karma—people who drain our energy and obligations that no longer make sense. "At 50," declared Penny Shore, " I now can choose how I want to live my life. Relationships and health are more meaningful. Time is such a valuable resource, I just don't want to waste it on things that don't matter." Hope Sealy, now 62, also felt that way. "I had a sense of who I was and what I liked. I stopped saying to myself, 'You don't like it, but you should try it.' I didn't care if a novel won the Pulitzer Prize; I no longer felt I had to be in by reading the latest book. And I stopped inviting people I felt obliged to entertain, especially if I felt the motivation was only a dry courtesy. I found it easier to choose how I wanted to live."

A patient told me a "freedom at 50" story that I can easily relate to. "Making the perfect dinner for guests drove me crazy," she admitted. "I lay awake all week planning the menu and rehearsing the timing of each course. I was so busy in the kitchen after my friends arrived that conversation was always interrupted and superficial. I never really listened or learned what was going on in their lives. Then something shifted at 50. I realized that we were getting together to fill our hearts with friendship and sharing, not to fill our stomachs. While I haven't resorted to hot dogs, I have changed my priorities. I no longer fret over the menu, foods are simpler, and much of it is prepared in advance."

"Living in the moment requires getting rid of the clutter in your life," says author, counsellor, and speaker Pearl Cassel. "I

I carry a book with me at all times so I can read, relax, and not worry about waiting or delays.

Marilyn, sales consultant

don't allow physical or mental clutter. Any garbage is immediately removed from my house two to three times a day. If things come into my mind that I analyze as being unwanted, or toxic to my positive thinking, I dismiss them. I will not provide space in my mind to situations, people, or thoughts that won't pay the rent!"

If, when we are 50, the door to freedom and choosing how to live is slightly ajar, by the time we are in our seventies, it has swung wide open. By then we've had a lot of practice. Active businesswoman Ethel Scholl, 75, explained the unburdening process very succinctly: "You get to a certain stage in life and say 'I am going to please me.' I am not going to take on anything that aggravates or upsets me. You earn that through the aging process. When you're younger, you do a lot of things you don't want to do, but are supposed to do. Now I can say 'To hell with it!'"

June Callwood and Doris Anderson feel the same way as Ethel. "I used to run from one appointment to another, always feeling backed up with too many things to do." said June. "I needed more time for myself. Now, when I am asked to sit on a board or give a free speech, I say no. I have a greater sense of defining my limits and appreciating time than I used to." Doris tried opera and didn't like it. She does not feel obligated to go. "You can forget the things that you should do, like belonging to certain clubs or putting up with certain people."

I can always count on author Helen Weinzweig, 83, to speak openly about life. She uses the phrase "downward path to wisdom" to describe her journey. "Old age means downward—teeth and gums require your attention, your eyesight is not as good, walks you take are shorter. However, I enjoy total freedom. Time now is mine. It doesn't belong to doing the right things, or being at the right place, or looking after the right people. There are no returns on time spent, so I've become very greedy about how I spend my time." Helen then offered this pearl of wisdom that we should remember: "We all have choice, but many of us don't

I make my husband laugh every morning.
                                    Penny, health charity director

know it. We often subscribe to what everyone will approve of. If you can stand up to disapproval, to non-acceptance, to being isolated—this is freedom and being true to yourself. When you are old, there are no risks. You can get away with anything. You have permission to behave naturally!"

Not so easy to do, is it? But at 50 we still have time to get it right. In the meantime, we can start small to make choices that simplify our life.

EAR-RINGS. Your cellphone is not an appendage hanging from your ear, so don't treat it like one! Keep it out of restaurants and theatres. Unplug your telephone when you do not want to be disturbed. A patient of mine has a technique to ensure he doesn't check his messages while on vacation with his family: He changes his message to say that his mailbox is full, so he knows he won't receive any.

DE-CLUTTER, DE-SOONER, DE-BETTER! Start with one small chore, like sorting out your shoes and boots. Give those pointy-toed four-inch heels to the nearest teenager. Next, tackle your junk drawer in the kitchen. (Everybody has one.) My friend Bertha recently bought a new computer for her home office. She quickly realized she first had to clean out her entire office in order to make it fit. After a full day of sorting and throwing out enough paper to fill several garbage bags, she felt liberated. "I haven't cleaned my office in 13 years," she admitted. "I brought in one new thing and it motivated me to clean out ten times as much!"

R.S.V.P. (REJECT S'IL VOUS PLAÎT). Every time you receive an invitation, ask yourself: Do I really want to go? How important is this relationship to me? Is there something else I'd rather be doing instead? Am I saying yes out of obligation or will I feel guilty if I say no? Sometimes, even when we don't want to go, we need to do the right thing to support and help others, but otherwise we have to learn to say no, especially when we have so little valuable time for ourselves.

FIND YOUR DREAM TEAM. How much is your time and

I work productively at home in the mornings to avoid the stress of sitting in rush-hour traffic, then I leisurely drive to the office.
                                                        David, salesperson

energy worth? Hire people who can do it better, faster, and more easily than you. On occasion, hiring a cleaning lady, tailor, or gardener can greatly reduce your stress level. A session with a personal trainer can keep you motivated and fit.

ME-TIME. Sitting in the backyard studying cloud formations is not wasting time. Contemplation, meditation, and taking a slow walk are all healing ways to keep us peaceful and in the moment. Now you'll have to excuse me: I'm about to treat myself to a nap—my guilt-free choice for health and happiness!

DOING THE RIGHT THING

It's one thing for people like author Helen Weinzweig, at 83, to no longer be concerned with looking after the right people or doing the right thing. But what if you are in your middle years and coping with an aging parent? For Rifka Silverberg, 50, life for the past 15 years has consisted of daily phone calls, frequent visits, and trips with her mother to doctor's appointments. "Looking after my 86-year-old mom is part of my cell structure. Although she is still fairly independent, I do worry about her. My freedom is limited, particularly if I plan a vacation. I carefully weigh the distance I'm travelling and how long I'm away from her." Recently Rifka and her husband, David, visited Switzerland for one week. They rented a cellphone in case of an emergency. While they were hiking at 6000 feet in Interlaken, the phone rang. Rifka froze, fearing the worst. It was a wrong number. Her mother reassured her upon her return: "I'm still here. You shouldn't worry so much."

Because I don't have children, my responsibilities are vastly different from those of my brother Steven. At 53 he has four sons (two married and two teenagers). Mileage for him used to be how far he ran in the morning. Now it means the distance he drives taking wheelchair athlete Joel, 15, to compete in a tennis tournament

Every morning I make a point of chatting with my neighbours.
                                        Patrick, sound recordist

or chauffeuring Adam, 13, to the golf course or baseball practice. Although he will be retiring from his job later this year, he will still be busy juggling at least six roles—consultant, husband, father, grandfather, community leader, and board member of his synagogue. When our mother was in a seniors' residence six years ago, and then later a nursing home, it was Steven who visited her almost daily. I was thankful that he lived in the same city as Mom and that his office was nearby. He always made the effort and never complained.

We know that life is unpredictable. Just when we feel we finally have time to stretch out in the hammock and enjoy life, along comes a surprise. That's what happened to Robert Craig, now 54, who these days is busy diapering his twins, a boy and a girl. "I thought my fifties would be more laid back and relaxed," Bob explained, laughing. "Now I just can't see my life without kids. Do you know how wonderful it is to start each day with two happy two-year-olds who are so excited to see you?"

There is no one single scenario for obligations after 50. You might be at the stage where you are no longer pleasing kids or parents. Or you may be looking after teenagers or elderly parents at home, or supporting young adults who have returned to the nest or who've never left. Perhaps you are putting kids through university or coping with elderly parents in a nursing home.

Two years ago Bill Brissenden, 84, a widower for four years, moved into his son's home. "Dad was very unhappy living alone, so he moved in with my wife and me and our two young children," said Robert, 44. "The arrangement has worked out well for all of us. We eat dinner together every evening and he's become a built-in babysitter. He just loves the kids and they seem to keep him feeling younger." Addendum: "Dad slipped this morning on the porch and fell down three stairs. We took him to emergency and they are still assessing him. It's a worry."

Stress levels soar with any change in family situations, especially when you find that your personal time is reduced or your financial

I have a big bowl of organic fresh fruit—kiwi, strawberries, and raspberries—topped with yoghurt.

Ellen, consultant

obligations increase. A large measure of patience is vital when you find yourself in a role reversal, such as parenting your parents. As I wrote in a poem, "Life's Cycle": *Our parents become our children, in addition to our own, ...Mom, take your umbrella; are you eating well? Hold onto my arm; remember when you fell?*

I remember two things my mother said to me: (1) Who is going to look after you in your old age if you don't have children? And (2) I don't want to be a burden to you and Steven. When is a parent a burden? The answer is in your heart. Only you know if you are acting out of love and caring or are feeling trapped, unappreciated, or used. One of my patients is deeply resentful of and angry with her sister, who has walked away from any caregiving responsibility for their ill, aged mother. "She'll run back, of course, when the will is probated," she said.

Every situation is different. Only you can decide on limits, ground rules, standards, and what doing the right thing means to you. Is your 25-year-old living with you? Do you pick up his bills as well as his dirty clothes? Does he help with meals? One patient has agreed to pay for her daughter's three years of university. "But graduate school? She's on her own!" A recent study on "boomerang kids" found that the cluttered nest can be quite harmonious. Most parents preferred having their children with them, and mothers in particular valued the companionship.

So how do you find a balance between having a life and having guilt? Each of us must choose what we are willing to do for someone—and why. How do you repay your parents for all the years they looked after you? When a parent needs you, are there any limits? How do we find joy in these responsibilities? I asked Maureen Sheedy, 61, who with her sister Pat is looking after their 95-year-old mom, now in a nursing home. "I visit with her for several hours, three times a week, not to mention the hours spent in the hospital when she was recovering from a fractured pelvis and hip after one of her falls. If she was mean and nasty, it would be a good reason not to visit as often. But Mom has always been a

I write thank-you notes to people every day to show my appreciation for things big or small.

Eveleen, volunteer

very sweet lady, never controlling. I've never resented what I've had to do for her. She's my mother."

OUR ALBATROSS

In Samuel Taylor Coleridge's poem "The Ancient Mariner," an old man describes how he shot an albatross with his crossbow when he was a young sailor. The seabird had guided his storm-driven ship out of the Antarctic. When trouble then befell the ship, the crew blamed him for it. They hung the dead bird around his neck as a curse. The phrase "an albatross around the neck" has come to denote a burden, particularly one that is difficult to get rid of.

All of us carry burdens from our past. Their heaviness has also been expressed as "carrying the weight of the world on one's shoulders." No wonder I treat so many patients for neck and shoulder pain! In my poem "Use the Good Dishes" I write about life's lessons: "Be grateful for the rough ones, the pain and the tough ones, everyone has their turn." No one is spared emotional pain and upheaval—loss, hurt, fear, inadequacy, resentment, jealousy, anger. There is no timetable for their arrival in our life, and their departure depends on us.

Some people resolve their issues; some never do. I know of a woman whose marriage ended 25 years ago. She is as angry with her ex-husband today as she was when her marriage ended. She never remarried, and barely acknowledges him at family functions. Special arrangements are always made in advance to make sure they don't visit the grandchildren at the same time. The husband let go of his anger decades ago and is healthier for it. She colluded with the albatross. This bitterness fuels and propels her, it's her cause, her torch, her raison d'être. The enemy has been very convenient and useful for two reasons: She always has someone to blame for her miserable life, and she is not compelled to take any responsibility for the breakup. Sadly, she will remain scornful forever.

Every morning I sit in my favourite coffee shop, read the paper, and watch people.

Monica, hairdresser

I consulted a psychiatrist friend to learn more about unburdening. "The past makes us what we are today—good, bad, or indifferent," he said. "And everybody has baggage—we can't be raised without it. Some people's baggage doesn't get in the way of them living a normal life. Like a jockey carrying an extra 20-pound weight belt, we get used to the burdens we carry. However, if our burdens are too great, we may turn to drugs, alcohol, or inappropriate behaviour."

"So how do we get rid of the albatross?" I asked.

"Remember, we helped get it there, and the albatross stays with our involvement. We need to overcome it by understanding and working on it with therapy and support from family and friends. Even new and better experiences can help us overcome pain from the past."

In my motivational speeches, I regularly ask the audience the following question: "Have you ever gone through something that at the time brought you to your knees, and now years later you realize how much you grew after you made peace with and let go of the situation?" Smiles and nods of recognition abound. When we are in the middle of a tempest, we never see the calm on the outside, or believe that things will get better. I know this from personal experience. Thirteen years after my marriage ended, I feel thankful for who I've become. Initially consumed with hurt, anger, and revenge, I barely functioned on a daily basis. When I can't fix something, I immediately find someone who will. I needed a therapist who could fix my broken heart. For those who fear therapy, making that first phone call is often the toughest. Once a week I would talk, cry, listen, and cry. I thought, "These 'tip of the iceberg' sessions could take years!" I wanted the advanced, deep-to-the-*kishkas*, accelerated program. So I shipped myself off to Esalen, a healing retreat in California. For two solid weeks I immersed myself in group discussions, crying, meditation, and one-on-one counselling. I even pounded pillows and screamed during a Gestalt therapy session. Emotionally spent, I returned home, ready to focus on healing rather than blaming.

I ride horses with my family on the weekend.

Adam, engineer

Two of the "cures" for the burdens I carried were accepting and appreciating—accepting loss or hurt, and appreciating the good things in my life. I couldn't see this until I worked through my anger and pain. Girlfriends with patient ears and the passage of time have both contributed to the process of letting go. I banished my albatross and feel twenty pounds lighter!

Our life history affects our physiology over time. That pain in the neck you're experiencing could be someone you live with or work with. In my 22 years as a chiropractor, I've treated many patients who drag in more than just sore butts! I've noticed that family rifts are often particularly gut-wrenching for most people. One patient described her path to healing: "My brother and sisters perceived that I was the favourite child. I was the youngest of four, and because of the significant age differences, I was still young when they grew up and moved away from the family farm. I was really raised as an only child. After I got married my husband and I helped my parents with their fruit business. I loved the farm but my siblings didn't seem to care about it. When my parents died, the three of them received money and I inherited the farm and business. They have always been jealous and resentful, and there have been times when we were not speaking at all. I've made peace with myself and only partially with them. I am not responsible for what my siblings are still holding onto. That is their burden."

A poor self-image is a familiar demon for many. Disliking the body you live in—feeling too short, too tall, or too heavy—can be a huge encumbrance. It wasn't until David Talbot got married and had children that he was finally able to stop feeling uncomfortable with his body image—a burden he had been carrying since grade five swimming class. "I was always a skinny kid, constantly reminded by my mother and grandmother, 'You're so skinny, you don't eat enough!' It rings in my ears like the Liberty Bell. The worst time of my life was swimming nude with other ten-year-old boys. I was always the skinniest. In those days, if

I bike to my local coffee hangout and meet my friends.

Jerry, policeman

you didn't look like Charles Atlas, kids thought you were a wimp. So this inhibition plagued me right through high school and into university." How did he finally shed the albatross? "At some point, I think in my mid-twenties, I made a conscious decision that it was no longer important. Carrying this burden from age 10 to 25 was long enough. I just let it go." Now 59, this strategic planner with excellent posture and good health remarked, "When I look around at so many overweight people, I feel blessed to be lean!"

Sharon Allen, an art gallery director in La Jolla, California, found that history kept repeating itself until she finally learned to let go of the past. She related three different stories—each involving regret, some degree of loss, and anger. About ten years ago, she was in a relationship with a man who died in a freak car accident. "Unfortunately we had had an argument two weeks earlier and hadn't spoken. I didn't have a chance to say goodbye to him. For two years, I beat myself up over this. If I had only...." Through grief therapy she was able to move on. Then her home was burglarized, and she was heartbroken over the loss of her jewellery. Finally, she got mixed up in a love-business relationship with a charming man who turned out to be a pathological liar. "I discovered that he had been using our money for illicit purposes. I confronted him and he attacked me and put me in a stranglehold. I grabbed a silver vase and hit him over the head. He let me go, left the apartment, and called police. They bought his fabricated story and I was charged with felony and assault. I was arrested and spent three days in jail." The nightmare continued. Once released, Sharon learned that the sociopath had placed a restraining order on her so she couldn't return to their apartment. With only the clothes she was wearing and no money she called a friend, and he let her stay on his boat for a month. "I felt utterly helpless, weak, and desolate," she told me. "Then one night I looked up to the heavens and prayed to God for help. I just put everything in his hands. I could feel myself let go of the anger and the pain of my

I do volunteer work for charities.

                                    Walt, retired life insurance agent

whole existence." Sharon rebuilt her life after that. Her family helped her financially and she was able to get a good job.

"Things kept being taken from you," I suggested.

"Yes, but when I let go of all the negative emotions and material things that I gave power to, my life got better. My life has been all about growth—letting go and trusting the universe. When you unburden emotionally you understand this truth: The other side of pain is more consciousness and awareness."

Bernie Klein is one of the most aware individuals that I am privileged to know and love. He would laugh at this pronouncement, because modesty and humility are very much a part of who he is. Unburdening and letting go have been his watchwords since 1991. He went through a painful journey that saw him descend helplessly into the mire, but in his words, "In order to grow you have to sink to the depths of your being." A series of crises stripped him to the core. "Business reversals, issues with children, a crumbling marriage, and a bout with cancer pushed me to examine where I've been, where I am, and where I'm going. Until you are tested you never know how you'll deal with things." With tremendous inner strength and tenacity, he realized he had to face the past to begin the healing process. "If you don't let go of hurts, regrets, and anger, they will make you sick, physically and emotionally." With courage, he was open to receiving whatever help he needed to get well—therapy, support groups for cancer patients, healing retreats. A caring family was his lifeline, as were exercise, a vegetarian diet, journaling, and daily meditation. "The only way to live is in the present," he believes. "And to do that you must let go of the past. Healing is not done in a straight line. It's a process, an evolution. I've learned to forgive, to be less judgemental, to be more compassionate." For the past four years that we've been together I have lauded his healing path as he journeys towards equanimity, acceptance, and love for himself and others. If we are all here on this planet to heal, love, and learn from each other,

I park my car 20 minutes away from my office so I can enjoy a walk up a hill in the morning and downhill at the end of my day.
                                                              Jeff, banker

then I feel truly blessed to have Bernie's hand to hold as I journey forward on my path.

IF ONLY...

In Roman mythology, Janus, the god of portals or doorways, is
depicted as having two faces. When Janus stands in the doorway
he looks forward and backward at the same time—seeing where he
has been while keeping his eyes focused on where he is going.
On which direction are you focused? Are you able to look back at
the past, remember experiences that are part of who you are,
extract the lessons learned, and move forward with gratitude into
the future? Or do you keep looking back, stuck in the bog of "if
only," regretting missed opportunities, the paths you chose, or
the relationships that didn't work out? Regret is akin to plaque nar-
rowing the flow of joy that courses through our hearts every day.
Guilt, sadness, hurt, and misery ensue, making regret the biggest
burden of all.

If you could return to any point in your life and change a decision that you made, would you? Why? This question allows us to
press the rewind button on our life histories as we reflect on our
choices. For an instant we can consider all the major decisions that
comprise our journey—relationship choices, career choices, education and family decisions, choices that affect our health. Your
answer speaks volumes about regret, hindsight, acceptance, and
your current capacity for joy and equanimity.

I asked adults of all ages to consider this question and here
are the results:

Sixty percent of the respondents said yes, they would definitely change a decision they had made. Issues involved relationships, education, career, having children, and health. Here are
some actual replies:

*I listen to children's music. It's happy, playful, and filled with a sense
of wonder.*

Nadine, teacher

Relationship regrets:
- I should have stayed with my spouse. The grass is not greener.
- I should have married my boyfriend and not listened to my parents.
- I should have said no when my ex-husband asked me to marry him.
- I never told my father how much he meant to me. Now he's gone.
- I married too young. I wish I had listened to my parents.
- I wish I could repair my relationship with my father. We don't speak.

Career/education regrets:
- I left school to go into banking. I should have gone to university.
- I made a mistake by going into nursing.
- Instead of starting my own career/business, I became a housewife.
- I became a teacher, though I would have loved landscape design.
- I should have taken a year off to consider all career options.
- I should have stayed in school instead of getting married.
- I chose the profession my parents wanted, not what I wanted.

Children and regrets:
- I wish I had children, but I married too late.
- I wish I had waited to have children.
- I wish I had kept the child I gave up for adoption.
- I wish I hadn't had an abortion.

Health regrets:
- I wish I had never started smoking.
- I should have made health a priority.
- I wish I had seen a doctor sooner.

Each day I read from a daily devotional booklet to connect me with my spirituality.

Gertha, *retired businesswoman*

Maturity and regrets:
- I wish I had had the confidence to pursue a career in sports.
- I should have followed my intuition and my dreams, but I wasn't confident enough.

These regrets make me realize that sometimes we had no choice. Often parents dictated our direction in life. As well, we are all human, and make mistakes. Often it is not the choice that is problematic but the way we feel about a choice we made. If you are torturing yourself with regret, why not try to change your future? For example, you can choose to further your education by taking courses or going back to school. If you truly want to, you can make a concerted effort to find your passion, change your career, make health a priority, or quit smoking. As for the most difficult relationship regrets, stop looking back over your shoulder. Forgive yourself and others and ultimately accept what is.

Forty percent of the respondents said no, they would not change any decisions they had made. Here are their reasons:

- Although the road has been challenging and bumpy, I am truly happy where I am and with who I have become.
- All decisions were based on my best and considered judgements at that time. I don't dwell on the mistakes or what ifs.
- It is not only the decisions we make but how we adapt to changing circumstances. I trust the universe.
- It is my philosophy to not carry any regrets. I have learned to count my blessings and have made many "right" decisions in my life.
- I believe that life's journey is meant to teach us the lessons we uniquely need to learn.
- All that I have gone through has made me the person I am today. Divorce was difficult, but I have three wonderful children.
- I believe that the decisions I have made were necessary to

If I feel angry with someone, rather than hold onto it, I send good thoughts their way.

Shernaz, executive asistant

get me to this point in my life, which is exactly where I am supposed to be. I accept that with equanimity.

Without hesitation, I too would answer "no" to this question. My life so far has been a fascinating story with a cast of a thousand characters and many chapters still to be written. Although there is much in my book on relationships—marriage, divorce, past and present lovers, and deciding not to have children—I have absolutely no regrets about my journey. Though in my twenties and thirties I could not have articulated these thoughts, I now have a deep sense of trust in the meaning and purpose of my life. I understand that my choices were the right ones for where I was emotionally at that moment in time. If we value the process of life, then whatever path we take is the right one for the learning we need. However, when we are in the midst of pain, suffering, hurt, or loss—all of which I have experienced—it is almost impossible to see how any of it can be useful or good. In our own way and on our own timetable, we must struggle to come to terms with our decisions. The further removed we become from the rawness, the easier it is to see the meaning, the purpose, and the lessons.

Artist Doris McCarthy, who is almost 90, can look back a very long way, like Janus the Roman god, and guide us on our path. "I keep my eye on the half of the bottle that is full and ignore the half that is empty. The half that is full is so rich, so rewarding, so happy, that I would be stupid to regret the things I haven't had." Advice from Mary Thomas, 86: "I have no regrets. Don't drag anything behind you on a chain. Make peace with the past and the decisions you made."

Deborah Szekely, 77, founder of the famous Rancho La Puerta Spa in Baja, California, uses the following method to make choices in her life. "Every choice in life, whether it is about food or lifestyle or even thoughts, is either life-enhancing or life-diminishing. Just tag it. Look at it and say, 'Is this going to diminish

I love watching my cat wrestle with my two schnauzers.

Ruth, nurse

my life or enhance it?' Sometimes you just have to say, 'I can't do much about it,' forget it, and go on to things that are life-enhancing. Remember, you are building a reservoir of happiness. Why counterbalance it with unhappiness?"

I love the quote from novelist and poet Herman Melville on mishaps, which I think applies equally to regret. "Mishaps are like knives that either serve us or cut us, as we grasp them by the blade or by the handle." Remember: We learn from both the safety of the handle and the gashes from the blade. Never regret either.

Let It Go

Not what I ordered, stuck on hold,
noisy neighbours, berries with mould,
flights delayed, hey! that's my space,
more than ten items, lost suitcase,
talking in movies, plumber's a no-show,
ill-mannered kids, this line is too slow,
another voice mail, doctor is late,
sick on vacation, rising prime rates,
a missing sock, credit card bills,
out of toilet paper, traffic standstill,
cheque's in the mail, freezing rain,
computer glitch, more weight gain,
reservation lost, cancelled dates,
he's in a meeting, teens aggravate,
broken promises, little white lies,
petty arguments, eye for an eye.

The world isn't perfect, neither are you.
Forgive others and yourself for what you do.
Life is a hassle if you let it be, my friend.

If I smile at a stranger and they smile back, I feel joyful.
Rick, social worker

Focus on the good things, I recommend.
Each day has a natural rhythm and flow.
See the cup half full, let the negatives go!

I took some time last year for personal reflection during the ten
days between Rosh Hashanah and Yom Kippur, the most important Jewish holy days. On Yom Kippur we ask forgiveness from our
family, friends, and others for any harmful acts, slights, insensi-
tivities, or injustices committed in the previous year. The primary
feature of Yom Kippur is the Confession involving 56 categories
of sin. One of them, "the sin we have committed against You
[God] in our thoughts," refers to all the judgements, criticisms, and
negative, petty thoughts that infiltrate our mind and fill our day.
Although the holy days serve as a once-a-year remembrance to forgive ourself and others, we need weekly and daily reminders to let
go of trivial issues and negative thoughts that prevent us from
being open to the wonder, surprise, and joy of everyday life. Many
of us aren't even conscious of these negative thoughts. While we
may be aware of the importance of letting go of the big burdens in
our life, we must also learn to let go of the small, everyday, exas-
perating frustrations that can drain our energy and instantly steal
our joy.

If our brains produced a printout of our thoughts at day's end,
we'd likely be horrified at the huge number that are negative.
What do you think these thoughts do to you? "I just bought this
milk and it stinks! What a rip-off!" "That **** idiot! He waits 'til
the light is green and then decides to put his signal on!" "Damn!
It's raining. What a lousy day!" Bad moods have a way of escalating. Someone cuts you off in traffic and the next thing you
know you take it out on the nearest person—snapping at your
assistant at the office or at a family member. Be conscious of your
negative thoughts. Do you too often use the word "but" to bridge
two thoughts? As in "The party was great, but the food was better
last year" or "The movie was good, but the popcorn was too salty"

I give myself a manicure and a pedicure every week.

Lily, consultant

or "She looked terrific, but I didn't like her hair." When we are consumed with finding fault or magnifying what isn't working in our life, we can't pay attention to or appreciate the surprises and unexpected joyful things that also happen every day—hearing a wonderful joke that makes you laugh, being told to "go ahead of me" in line, or getting a spontaneous hug from your kids.

Thinking positively can also turn a potentially embarrassing error into an unexpected opportunity. At one of my recent speaking engagements, the sign outside the conference room was supposed to read "Health and Wellness." Instead, in beautiful calligraphy, someone had written "Health and Wettness." Was I annoyed? No. I laughed and removed the sign before the audience arrived, and the manager apologized and replaced it. This was the perfect opening for my speech. The all-female audience howled with laughter when I said that whoever had made the sign must have thought there were a bunch of menopausal women in the room having hot flashes! We need to laugh more and fret less.

HOW MUCH IS ENOUGH?

Forest Hill is an exclusive residential area in mid-Toronto dotted with expansive old trees and expensive old homes. My office is located there, framed by million-dollar dwellings and spacious flowering gardens. Some of Forest Hill's residents are my patients. (Rich or poor, back pain is an equal-opportunity affliction.) I was invited to a luncheon for 250 women in one of those homes, full of priceless paintings and oriental carpets. A long marble walkway led me to a room the size of a conference centre! This solarium contained an indoor pool with a uniquely designed cover that converted the pool area into a floor. How many people do you know with the space and money to host a catered sit-down lunch for 250 in their home? After the luncheon, while I waited for the valet service to retrieve my car, I reflected on the emotional costs

Every day I speak to someone I love.

Marianne, psychologist

of maintaining that lifestyle. How much time is devoted to family, and how much to work, or to ego? How much opportunity is there for quiet reflection? Is balance possible for any of us? What is a successful life? And how much stuff is enough?

Balance is a concept that is as difficult to achieve as it is to define. To me it is about the choices we make in life, our priorities and what gives us meaning. Michael Adey, a mentor, taught me 30 years ago that we are what we do, not what we say. There are often huge gaps between what people say they think is important and how they actually spend their time.

I know what it is to be totally out of balance. I lived that way for about five years when I started to compete in marathons. My training came first and everything else, including my marriage, family, and work, came second. Though being focused helps you accomplish your goals, it takes a toll in terms of the time and energy you have left for nurturing yourself and others.

Many people who visit my office aren't aware that their lives are out of control until a pain stops them in their tracks. They may be raising families, and walking that precarious tightrope of push-pull, between wanting and having. How much is enough? They may believe that money will solve all their problems, but they still want it all—more money, more time with their families, and maybe a little time for themselves. Scott Cowie, 40, summed it up neatly: "Between 20 and 40, money means a whole lot, assuming of course you have your health. Beyond 40, the meaning in life shifts, especially if you start losing grandparents, parents, and friends."

According to psychotherapist Shelley Stein, we do not give enough thought to where we are expending our energy. "People don't say no enough or factor their own personal needs into the equation. They factor in their children's or supervisor's or husband's needs, but they don't think about themselves—me time. You need to say no in order to have balance." It makes sense to me that if one constantly pursues *more*, one will experience joy *less*.

I read my two newspapers every morning in my favourite chair with a cup of coffee.

Evelyn, businesswoman

Joy comes from inner peace and gratitude for what one has, not from amassing wealth.

In a lecture I attended at Canyon Ranch Health and Wellness Resort in Arizona on the subject of balancing work and home, Dr. Robert Rhode, Ph.D. suggested that we create intimacy in our life. This requires emphasizing feelings, experiences, and memories instead of mastery, which is based on logic, intellect, and rationality. For example, a teen will go to a mall and just hang out. That is an intimacy experience. We will go to a mall with a mission—to buy what we want and get out of there. That is mastery. Mastery, the way many of us work, focuses on getting things done, the end goal, and being in control. Intimacy stresses the process, and asking yourself questions like "How did I connect with others today? What did I do to further my spiritual goals today? How far back do I have to go to savour a memory? What did I do today that had no goal, but that I enjoyed just as an experience?" Mastery individuals often forget or minimize birthdays, anniversaries, or holidays, focusing their energy instead on work-related issues. I hiked with many "mastery types" at the ranch. They march up the mountain with heads down, determined to maintain a specific heart rate, while others stop to inquire about a certain flowering cactus or to admire the beautiful view along the way. "We are used to annual reviews at the office," Rhode says, "but what about an annual review at home? How about putting down an intimacy goal in your appointment book or daytimer, like, 'Find out something new about my spouse or teen today.'"

If "only our hairdresser knows for sure," then Robert Gage learns a great deal while he snips and coifs the locks of the rich and famous. I asked, "How much is enough?" "Ten or twenty million is like a drug for some of my clients," he said. "You become more and more wired to having more money. When money interferes with your life, when it takes you away from meaningful things and the people you love, it is enough." Robert feels that most of our immediate problems can be solved with money. "However,

I like to make people laugh in the middle of a serious business meeting.
Phil, CEO

the problem with having too much is that you're not sure whether people like you or agree with you only because of your wealth." I liked Robert's candour when he added, "Poverty sucks also." Robert seems to have found a perfect balance in his own life. He works four days a week in the city, and has three days off to relax at his country home. "My three days off make me happier than any amount of money I could make on that fifth day. I have learned to enjoy each day and make today a wonderful experience whether I am cooking, gardening, entertaining or visiting friends, or listening to music."

Lawyer Joseph Sorbara, 57, who is involved in a family business, has redefined what a successful life means for him. "Each year as I get older, I find that material things are less important. I used to get a kick out of going to my tailor and ordering three suits. Well, it just doesn't do anything for me any more." Remarried now with two young children, he has felt a growing need for solitude. "I used to feel guilty about taking time for myself, not wanting my wife and family to interpret this as a slight to them. Now I see this as a necessity—a recovery mechanism in order to go forward." To balance his busy work and home life, he takes about an hour each day for quiet reflection. "In the summer I'll go down to my boat in the middle of the week, sit on the back deck, put my feet up, and look out at the water. Sometimes I think about nothing but how peaceful and wonderful it is to be here." I asked Joseph how much is enough. "My thinking used to be that time is money. Now I believe that time is life! A meaningful life is not about the dollars you have in the bank, or how good a business deal you made because you got the better of the other side. It is about relationships—relating to a fellow human being in the context of love and friendship. It is about honour, respect, and helping one another."

Steve Burns has a close working relationship with the almighty dollar. A busy accountant, he helps clients make, organize, and save money. "There are always clients who measure their value as

I speak to my two-year-old grandson every day on the telephone.
Bonnie, manager

a person by how much money they make or accumulate. All of their energy is devoted to that end. 'More chips in the game of life'—that is how they keep score. Friendship, the people you help, the number of times you smile each day, the number of times your eyes become misty because you've been emotional or something touched you—to me, these are the successes in life."

Ben Orenstein, 78, a former CEO in the hospitality industry, founding chairman of Harbourfront Corporation, and a member of a number of community organizations, truly enjoys his life. "Everyone has different aspirations and goals. I love to ski, sail, and travel. I have been fortunate enough to help charitable organizations, including various hospitals and the university. What impresses me are people's achievements in business or the community. The measurement of a successful person is a history of achievement, not the money they have."

Hal Jackman, 67, has been chairman of many companies and organizations, chancellor of the University of Toronto, and lieutenant-governor of Ontario. I asked him about reaching the corporate pinnacle and whether balance refers strictly to accounting sheets. "CEOs devote their entire lives, their energy, their everything to their work," he admitted. "Instead of having a close family life and a supportive circle of friends, they only have colleagues and business clients. Then, when they are replaced, they go back to a wife they hardly know, and have no outside interests. They don't know what to do with the rest of their lives." This scenario doesn't sound like fun to me (although owning a corporate jet might save me some travelling time!). When that CEO drives home in his Mercedes, no one really cares if he's there or not.

No matter how much we know better, society still equates money with power, status, and success. I love Oscar Wilde's line, "Nothing succeeds like excess." My dad, lecturing Steven and me on the pursuit of wealth, would say, "You can only wear one pair of pants at a time!" But why limit yourself if you can afford not to? Many of the people who told me that money wasn't meaningful

I remember some personal thing that a co-worker tells me so I can ask them about it next time and make them feel special.
                    Tahir, telecommunications specialist

to them have a million times more than just enough. I wonder if they'd feel the same if they had half of the money they do. Bernie Klein, an entrepreneur who understands the difference between red and black, explained it to me this way: "It's often the people who can really afford it who say, 'Money isn't that important.' It's like someone going on a luxury safari and saying, 'Gee, I'm living in the wilderness,' except they have 85 security guards protecting them. They are surrounded by total comfort and safety. They may be in the wilds, but they're really in a gilded cage."

"So how much is enough?" I asked him.

"It takes real work, real thought, real strategy to have a meaningful balance. Money, without love, friendship, learning, and satisfaction with what you do, is meaningless. So many people just *talk* about balance, but they don't go deeply enough and actually modify their lives. Taking your kids to school each day instead of showing up early at the office is a choice. You must prioritize what is important to you and carry it through. Money should be treated as a resource, not an end goal. Success in life is not wealth or power. It is about who you are, not what you have."

And who you are defines what "enough" is for you. Everyday life may be plenty for some; others need more to feel complete. More importantly, once you decide *who you want to become*, you'll know how much is enough.

I go to my health club first thing in the morning and work out.
                                                        Gilles, pilot

REMEMBERING

The Fridge Door

If you want to understand me, read my fridge door,
A microcosm of my life, this square on the floor.
A bulletin board with magnets holding up notes,
Kids' drawings, appointment cards, and important quotes.
Photos of my family, the kids grow so fast!
I removed last year's boyfriend, he's history, in the past.
Here's one of me I like. Was I a little thinner?
This recipe for chicken, a guaranteed winner.
A date with the vet for my furry feline friend;
My psychotherapist's number, take it, I recommend.
A wedding invitation, another one from *her*—
She says she's got it right this time; I'm really not so sure.
A grocery list, so I don't miss that one important item.
My lawyer's cellphone number, mustn't talk ad infinitum.
A cartoon on chiropractic a patient sent by fax,
An article on Type A's—that's me! (I must relax.)
I love this artist's drawing from Joel, who's almost eight—
That's how Picasso started. With lessons he'll be great.
My cleaning lady's number, not sure if I should call her—
She missed behind the couch. For that it's 80 dollars?
This magnet of a pig eating chocolate cake,
When I really feel like bingeing, it makes me hesitate
To explore the shelves of treats that are enticing me.
They should make locks for all fridge doors,
I'd throw away my key.
A column from Ann Landers, my Mom clipped out for me.
It's yellowing with age, but full of memories.
Whenever I need help I read Ann's little saying;
That's what my Mom would do, plus a little praying.

I have some distant memories that really take me back.
I'd say "Hi, Mom. What's for dinner? Can I have a snack?"
I'd stand with door ajar to view the goodies in it,
"You're letting out the cold. Close the door this minute!"
Now there's no one in my kitchen, save for me
and my fridge door,
And the memories of childhood and Mom forevermore.

Whether it's "use the good dishes," "look to this day," or "carpe diem," this fundamental advice is often ignored. Age allows some wisdom in this, to see that today is important, as you see people die, children grow in a flash, and opportunities pass by.

I suppose my good dishes these days are people. I feel lucky for all the time I can spend with my parents, who are still in good form. Golfing with my mother (we are both pretty bad), for the beauty of the day, for the enjoyment of an occasional good shot, or just for the laughs. After a lifetime of avoiding it, I've started fishing with my dad (an expert) and love seeing the look on his face when he hooks one. I used to watch my daughter in her sleep before she went to university, much like I did when she was a baby. I remember thinking that once she left for school, she would never be part of family life in the same way again.

My husband and I go out for dinner, spend weekends exploring something new and try to travel by bicycle once a year so that we can go slow, smell the chestnut blossoms, and see the countryside.

I believe you have to take time for yourself—a bath, a book, a massage, a walk. Even buy yourself flowers. Sleep is a huge luxury, but when I'm away I'd rather get out and see or explore. You can always catch up on sleep later.

You have to see friends, make an effort, get together, drink wine (or champagne) and laugh.

Valerie Pringle

I fly my float airplane up north and go fishing.

Rick, pilot

THE WAY WE WERE

At one of my writing workshops on recording happy memories, John remembered his father. "It was the happiest trip of my life, and the last one my dad and I took together," John said, dabbing his eyes with Kleenex. "Dad was terminally ill with cancer. One morning he asked me to take him to Vancouver so he could see his eight-year-old grandson one last time. Though it was against doctor's orders, we went. During the five-hour flight, we reminisced, laughed, and bonded. I told him how much I loved him and that he was the best father." As John's voice broke, the Kleenex box was passed around to all the other CEOs at the table.

I begin these workshops by asking the group members to close their eyes, breathe deeply, and reflect on happy, cherished memories and outstanding experiences of their lives. "Think back to your childhood and the best times you ever had—family vacations, special birthdays, grandparents who were there for you, the home where you grew up, family pets, favourite teachers, toys, games and movies, school and sports achievements." Then I progress through the years: Driving a car, falling in love with that little red-haired girl, high school graduation, university days, your first full-time job, crazy, wild times, a marriage proposal, having children. I touch on many rites of passage and life transitions to awaken their memories. As I observe their faces, many of the men, with their eyes still closed, smile just thinking about their lives.

After five minutes, I instruct them to open their eyes. "Don't talk to anyone. Write down your happy memories as quickly as you can, with as many specific details as you can remember. No editing. Now, go!" Pens sprint and pages flip over. When the frenzy begins to wane, I ask them to choose one memory and share it with the others. At this particular session, the men chose "safe" subjects they could easily talk about—catching six trout and two mackerel on a first fishing trip with Dad, winning the cross-country championship in grade ten, the birth of a son and holding him for

Each night before we sleep my wife and I say to each other, "I love you because..." and we give a reason for that day.

Keith, pilot

the first time. When John spoke, his vulnerability and openness permitted the rest of the group to choose more profound events. This facilitator needed the Kleenex box, too! That whole experience is now recorded in my memory book.

All of us have experienced thousands of happy moments in our lives. Too often they remain buried under the rubble of the everyday worries and problems that take up space in our heads. We know that life hands us unhappy memories as well, but as psychotherapist Shelley Stein suggests, "We must honour all of our experiences, good and bad. Just don't dwell on the misery. Once you learn the lesson, you can let it go and not stay attached to negative memories." I often imagine that we have an attic in our minds filled with happy memories. We need to open that rusty door, remove the cobwebs, and dig these treasures out. Don't wait for your family to prompt you with, "Remember the crazy time when we...."

Just how is memory preserved, anyway? We've all had awe-inspiring moments that psychologist Abraham Maslow calls "peak experiences"—profound moments frozen in time when we say, "I will always remember this." And we do. The signal to hold on to a memory originates in the hippocampus, a ridged structure in the brain. Over a period of weeks, some signals will magnify nerve cell connections and diminish others. Eventually you accumulate a permanent record of the memory that can be retrieved at a later time.

Driving home after clinic hours one evening, I was mesmerized by a huge, low-lying yellow moon. It was as if there was a magnetic force pulling me towards it; I could hardly focus on the highway as I stared in disbelief at the sheer enormity of this giant illumined saucer. With great excitement I pulled into my driveway and raced into the house. I grabbed my portable phone, and went outside again. I then called my parents, who lived in a small town about 40 miles away.

In my mind, I could picture the layout of their house and the direction they would have to face to view the moon with me.

Every Saturday I go to a garage sale to find one treasure.

Terri, artist

"Daddy," I directed, "take Mom's hand and go out the back door and turn right." I waited patiently for several minutes. Finally my dad returned to the phone and said, "It was nice, wasn't it!" It's funny the memories we cherish. But now that my mom and dad are gone, I'll always remember that magic moment when my parents and I were moonstruck together. Sharing the experience when we lived so far apart was special for me. And I opened their eyes to something they otherwise might have missed.

Dr. Pamela Letts

One effective way to help make a memory stick is to replay the event. Storytelling with family will preserve the past and can be especially important for younger members. Sylvia Molson, 80, feels strongly about this: "I tell my grandchildren stories about my parents. They love to hear about all the technological changes—horse and buggy days, washing clothes by hand and hanging them out on the line, having only one bathroom for 11 people in our house. There is no way my great-grandchildren will know about these and other special memories unless they are passed on through storytelling."

Our immune system benefits from happy memories as well. Whether we feel happy or sad, hormones released from the brain send messages to cells throughout the body. This crucial mind-body connection influences our health. Happy feelings increase the number of disease-fighting natural killer cells—our bodies' police force—which may help to explain why optimists are often healthier than pessimists. A memory book filled with life's cherished events is good for us. Even the process involved in writing memories down is beneficial for our hearts and souls. "It's important to revisit happy times," Dr. Robert Salter, 74, believes. "Many people go through life complaining that things are not going their way. I often say to them, 'There must be some happiness in your life.' Happy memories counterbalance the negative and remind us to be thankful."

I walk through the woods early in the morning with my dog.

Aileen, teacher

Sixteen years ago, on my birthday, my brother Steven surprised me with a poem he had composed entitled "Do You Remember?" highlighting our happy and often mischievous childhood experiences. I am so grateful to him for giving me this heartfelt gift. When I read the first one, "Breaking the margarine on the carpet," I roared. In the old days (when we ate this stuff!), white margarine had to be kneaded in its packet by hand to blend in the artificial colour. While my parents were out, Steven and I decided to play catch, throwing the packet back and forth across the living room and squishing it a bit to mix in the colour. Call me butterfingers! The packet smashed on the floor and split wide open, sending a wave of yucky, slippery guck all over the place. I'm laughing now as I write this, but you don't want to know the trouble we got into! Remember, we are focusing on *happy* memories!

Now it's your turn. Find a book or binder with blank pages and start your own memory book. Close your eyes and reflect on your joyful memories. When you are ready, start with these words: "I remember"—then begin writing. Here's a peek at one of my entries to get you going:

> *I remember my mother making me the gooo-iest, most delicious grilled cheese sandwiches, with two orange Kraft cheese slices on challah. That was my favourite lunch. She would butter the outside of the bread, put one buttered side down on the grill, wait for the magic sizzle, add the cheese, then add a piece of buttered bread on top. She knew just how I liked it. When the melted cheese squirted out from all sides, it was time to lift the lid. The last sound I always heard was my mom scraping the hardened bits of cheese off the grill.*

Allen Lambert, 89, the former chairman, director, and CEO of the Toronto Dominion Bank, shared some of his happy childhood

I love when I remember someone's name before I introduce them.
Richard, retired

memories with me. His kind eyes twinkled as he recalled, "On my birthday (which is December 28, three days after Christmas), my mother would bake me my very own Christmas cake. I was the only one out of seven kids to have this treat, so I never felt I was missing out on anything. My mother was very wise and she always did these little things for me to make me feel special. I also have a strong memory, from when I was four or five, of playing a lot in the breakfast room. We had oak chairs and a big table. All the kids would line the chairs up to look like a team of horses. We then tied them together with old rags, which became the harness, and pretended to drive them."

If memories get stuck, looking through old photo albums is a wonderful way to help them flow. Even our senses can trigger memories. Make a list of your favourite smells, tastes, and sounds, or what you love to gaze upon or touch. The smell of a peony (a flower my mother loved), the taste of summer beefsteak tomatoes (my father's favourite), or the song "You'll Never Walk Alone" (which we sang as a family) can instantly transport me on a magic carpet ride back to my childhood. I have over 500 delightful memories in my memory book, and continually add new ones.

Speaking of photo albums, many of us have photographs stuck in a drawer—just another job for our infinite to-do list. Not the Beder family. The wall of their family room is covered with thousands of snapshots representing their family's life. "We got the idea about 15 years ago to make a photo wall. If you put photos in albums, you have to make an effort to open them. This way our life is always on display for everyone to see. It's a great conversation piece. Every picture has a story. Here's one of me," Bobby said laughing, pointing to a childhood photo. "That picture was taken 57 years ago. My mother had me on a leash." Bobby walked me around the room, laughing and reminiscing as he highlighted pictures of his children, his grandparents, special vacation spots, and the family farm. The family room is running out of wall space, so the Beder family is thinking of starting a new photo room in

I get my hair done every week.

Marilyn, real estate agent

their house. After all, their daughter Alison just had their first grandchild!

When I was nine I dreamed of owning an electric train set. I hoped, even prayed, that my dad would buy me one for Christmas. On Christmas morning, I woke up before anyone and tiptoed downstairs to investigate the packages. There, under the tree, was a huge box with my name on it wrapped in green and red foil! I hesitated only briefly to consider the consequences, then ripped the paper off and lifted the lid. Joy of joys! It was the most beautiful train set in the whole world. In no time I assembled the cars and caboose and set them up on the gleaming silver track. All it needed now was power. I fiddled with the wiring on the power transformer and plugged the cord into the socket. A spark and a loud kaboom! ended the fun. I sat on the floor, scared, crying, and devastated. The commotion awakened my parents. Though my mom was visibly upset, I'll always remember the look on my dad's face—a half-smile of approval and exasperation rolled into one. "It's okay," he assured me, "we'll get you another one." Two days later, we drove into town for a replacement.

I'm a father now, with boys of my own. My 82-year-old dad just died last year. When I reflect on my childhood, two happy memories remain: That magic moment when I blew up my Christmas present, and the fact that I could always, always, count on my dad.

Keith, age 51

The wise, older adults who have provided a life map for my journey rejoice in their happy memories and celebrate family traditions and rituals. They feel an emotional connection to the past while honouring the present. In our fast-forward society, we spend much time planning, scheming, and daydreaming about the future. When we spend too much time looking forward, we neglect the richness of our own personal history. Life then becomes

Each month I create singing greetings on my answering machine to make people laugh when they call.

Marilee, teacher

meaningless, fragmented, and hollow. It is not enough to remember our rituals and traditions, we must keep them alive and pass them on to future generations.

THE FRIDGE

Whenever I visit friends and family, my favourite activity in the kitchen (besides eating) is reading the fridge door, that universal bulletin board. The fridge door is the home communication centre. It's a microcosm of life—a history of that particular home. The fridge door symbolizes what is truly important—family, friends, and life events that mark the passage of time. My girlfriend Sharon's fridge door is an upright photo album. There are more snapshots of people on that fridge saying "cheese" than there are people eating mozzarella at a pizza restaurant! I find it quite telling when a lonely fridge magnet or two are the only items clinging to the front of an otherwise naked appliance. Does anyone really "live" in that house, I wonder, when it seems that there is nothing personal they want to share? (Of course, I'll exempt those households with refrigerators that have non-magnetic doors, as long as a bulletin board is close by.)

For a quick update on life at my brother Steven's, I just start reading his family's fridge door. Currently, a large sheet entitled "Dembe Family Rules" is taped to the bottom half—five commandments to guide Joel and Adam. School photos, a calendar filled with lessons and sports activities, artwork, and a "For Better or Worse" cartoon strip overlap each other.

THE LIVING ROOM

I am going to instigate a revolution in your thinking and suggest that you rename a room in your home. The kitchen will now be

On Friday nights, we have a Sabbath service at home and then I bless my three children.

David, entrepreneur

called *the living room*. After all, how many of us actually "live" in the living room? Have you ever visited someone's home and noticed that there are no footprints on the living room carpet? No one has stepped in there for months. We often treat it as though it's for show, or for "good." Sometimes the couches or lampshades are covered with plastic. The place we really live in is the kitchen—the heartbeat of every home, the room that nurtures our souls and tickles our memories, and the place of gathering for family and friends. If a house were human, the kitchen would be the heart, the central focus of energy and life.

People are drawn to the friendliness, warmth, and comfort of kitchens. We've all had the experience of going to a party where small groups of people are chatting privately in the hallway or the dining room, while dozens of others congregate in the kitchen, squished against the counters but nevertheless feeling comfortable. And if you don't know many people at the party, it's often easier to initiate a conversation in a packed kitchen than to join an intimate group.

What is it about kitchens that makes us feel so *at home*? One possibility is that kitchens = food = love. Food has a psychological impact on all of us. From our earliest memories, food connected us to another human being. As infants we fed at the breast or bottle, lovingly caressed by our moms. Many of us came home from school greeted by wonderful smells in the kitchen—a roast chicken with potatoes or maybe a casserole (in the days when most moms stayed at home). I would often pop on the oven light, then kneel down and look through the glass window to see what was cooking.

Relationships were formed while eating together at the dinner table. "We had dinner together every night—all 11 of us," recalls Sylvia Molson, 80. "There were four girls, five boys, and our parents. Usually the biggest commotion was determining who was kicking whom under the table. My dad always sat at the head of the table, but the kids were allowed to sit anywhere. For me, eating

I hug and kiss my 18-month-old twins every morning.

                                                    Bob, broker

together was the happiest time." Unfortunately, for today's busy families, sharing a meal has become a challenge. These enduring memories of emotional nurturing associated with food are so vivid that people who live alone often eat in front of the television or while reading, just to have some kind of company.

In my mind's eye I can still see my mom making gefilte fish. She would lean against the kitchen counter, sometimes allowing me to turn the handle of the grinder, while she cautiously nudged the carp and whitefish closer to the rotating blades. Her famous tomato soup cake and meaty cabbage rolls serve as a gastronomic photo album and, years later, the aroma of special family and traditional foods can still rekindle a highly charged memory. Sylvia Molson cried the first time she made her deceased mother's gefilte fish. "Mom made the best fish. When I was first married she would come over and cook it at my house. It became a tradition that we all looked forward to. And my husband loved her cooking. After she died, I just couldn't bring myself to make it. There was such a strong connection to her." For many of us, food provides a sense of belonging to a family, or a cultural tradition, and a feeling of being connected to a larger whole, inextinguishable by time.

Last year, when her mother died, Denise Cherrington began the daunting task of cleaning out the entire contents of the family home where her 96-year-old mother had lived for 61 years. "There are a lot of foods I guess I won't be eating again," she lamented, glancing at the old Mixmaster, a relic from the 1930s. "Mom was a wonderful cook. We spent a lot of time in this kitchen watching her prepare preserves or make pastry. I've learned to make her grape conserves and her spicy chili sauce. But I'll miss her minced meat and the big Christmas puddings with brandy. Last week I found some old pickles in the cellar dating back to 1968. I opened the jar, removed the black ones, then tasted the ones underneath. They were so delicious, I ate the whole jar!"

So it's not just the food that nurtures us; we also develop a strong bond to the appliances, bowls, and dishes our parents used.

My husband and I set aside time each evening to share in each other's day.

Shelley, psychotherapist

Even your mom's cooking habits may be so engrained that you cook in exactly the same way. And it feels so normal and right that you balk at any other suggested method. When Carol Peterson was six, her mom received a waffle iron as a gift. "Mom made us waffles once a week for supper. It became our Saturday night treat." She laughed as she admitted, "Other women inherit jewellery, but I inherited my mom's precious waffle iron. Now I make the best waffles every Sunday morning. It's our ritual—a weekly reminder of my mom and a feeling of continuity with her life."

How can one measure the joy that Carol feels as she uses her mom's 44-year-old waffle iron during her weekly ritual, or Denise's happiness as she savours every bite of those 32-year-old pickles. It's impossible to put a value on the emotions invested in that pickle jar. How can I express how I feel each morning when I drink tea steeped in my father's 60-year-old one-cup teapot? He always added honey and milk to his tea. Is it surprising that I do, too? I find excuses to use my mom's 50-year-old jar lid opener, wanting to share the struggles she had when prying open a tight lid. These priceless kitchen treasures can nurture and sustain us while they connect us to all the significant people from our past.

The expensive items on display behind a cabinet's glass doors are not the real jewels in our life. What we cherish could appear worthless to others—like my mom's 50-year-old chipped mixing bowl, home to hundreds of cake mixes. How often did I lick chocolate from that bowl and the beaters? To me, it is a priceless memento of my childhood.

When was the last time you stopped to reminisce about or rejoice in the richness of your family traditions? Parents need to make rituals for their children. These rites are the threads in the fabric of life, connecting our past with the present. Get your family together and revive the traditions that may have been lost or forgotten, or start new ones. Dig out or re-create some recipes that you loved as a kid. And please, don't forget to invite me over for a cup of tea (milk and honey, please!) so I can read your fridge door in the "living room."

Every morning from May until October, I swim nude in my swimming pool.

Mollie, farmer

ACUTE NOSTALGIA

I am suffering from a bout of acute nostalgia. Every few minutes a wave of homesickness bounces between my heart and my gut. Medications won't help. Furthermore, this condition can be contagious, especially for the family who shares your memories. Reminiscing and the passage of time seem to be the best remedies.

Today is Mother's Day. Cars are double-parked outside Bob's Garden Centre just down the street from my house. My mom would have appreciated the gladioli, her favourite flower. I can almost hear her say, "Oh, Elaine, you shouldn't have." Then she would happily trim them and place each stem artistically in her crystal vase. She would also have enjoyed a mushy card with "Mom"—not "Mother"—printed on the front, because that's what I called her. She always checked the price on the back to make sure I hadn't spent too much money. (Moms have quirky habits like that.) Another ripple of homesickness just prompted me to send her an invisible "air mail" card with much love and remembrance, just by gazing up at the magnificent blue sky.

Homesickness can happen at any age. For Jane Ansin, 31, saying the word *homesick* triggers "an ache, a gnawing feeling in my heart." To lighten the emotional load, she likes to describe home as "just 24 hours away, by plane." (It's 16,358 km to her native New Zealand.) She calls her two-year work assignment in Canada a life-altering experience. "I now know how an alcoholic feels needing a drink. I fight with myself saying, 'Jane, you're not going to call them.' Then five seconds later I am dialing and saying, 'Hi, Mom.' Once I hear my family's voices I'm okay again. I also save my phone messages for a few days and play them back over and over again so I can hear them saying, "We love you and miss you." I've learned to value my family and friends so much more. Home is wherever there are people who love you."

Home is such a profound word. "Welcome home!" "Home at last!" "Are you going home for the holidays?" "Hi, Mom! I'm home!"

I enjoy making people smile with my jokes and happy attitude.
Millie, retired

Think about the emotional impact of those sentences. We all need to belong to a place, to call someplace "home." For some of us, home means where Mom and Dad live; for others it's our current address. *Home* also expresses an inner sense of belonging, a deep resonance in our hearts, a place we all started from, maybe the place where we grew up. "Home for me is my childhood with the big old house and veranda," recalled a 78-year-old judge. "I picture my whole family sitting together around the dinner table on Friday nights. My father was a salesman who travelled across the country, and Friday was the big day he came home. I would wait for him, anxiously looking out the window to see if he had arrived."

A house is not the same as a home. The words feel different when you say them. A house implies structure and shelter. With walls, doors, and windows, it's the physical embodiment of a home and only people can give it a spirit, a sense of warmth, comfort, and energy. "A home should tell a story about the people who live there," believes Pam Letts, a family physician in Florida. "Entering someone's home should give you a sense of who they are, what they've done with their lives, and what matters to them."

"When Fran and I were married 52 years ago, we built the first private house in a small community outside of Toronto," reminisced Judge Roger Conant, 77. "I laid the blocks for the foundation, hammered the roof, put on shingles. Our local minister, who was handy at electrical work, did the complete wiring. Our two boys were born there. Only in retrospect do I realize that those 12 years were the best part of our lives—the struggles of just starting out in life, feeling impoverished along with everyone else in the town. That was home to me."

Circumstances, particularly loss, often change where we call home. Now that my parents are deceased, *home* for me is Toronto. However, I will always have a strong emotional attachment to my childhood home on the "mountain" in Hamilton, where I lived from grade three until high school graduation. Sometimes I daydream about my family's nature hikes and berry-picking

I hug my three boys every morning before they go to school.
                                        Linda, mother

expeditions on the Bruce Trail. I'll always remember the magical tree house my father built, overlooking the brilliant fire-red sumac trees that dotted the hill behind our house. Two years ago I had an urge to return to that house. I introduced myself to the new owners, who were delighted to meet me and understood when I said that I just had to see my old bedroom. Slowly I walked that familiar route, down the hallway towards the main floor bathroom, then a left turn. Not surprising, I was struck by the room's smallness. As I looked out of the window I could barely reach when I was eight, I noticed one prominent reminder of the passage of time: Saplings my family had planted when we first moved there were now towering, mature oaks. I remember as a ten-year-old digging a hole (with my dad's help, of course) and planting a tiny willow tree about the same size as I was then. Some 41 years later, that willow had blossomed into a glorious beauty. I drove back to Toronto full of happiness, my acute nostalgia cured by a dose of wonderful memories.

It is precisely those precious memories—boxes and boxes of memories—that competitive athletes Brenda and Gary Baker are shipping to their new home in Whistler, British Columbia. They decided to follow their hearts and sell their Toronto home, where they've lived for 14 years. "We've labelled the boxes 'Memories/Storage.' They're filled with treasures like our kid's school mementoes, report cards, and class pictures, our family photographs, and running trophies. Half of our moving costs are devoted to preserving our family history." As for the remaining contents of their home, Brenda, commenting on their frequent garage sales, laughed, "We've spent eight weeks throwing out the junk we've collected for the last 14 years!" Emma, their seven-year-old daughter, just couldn't bring herself to say goodbye to her room. She has decided to buy back the house when she grows up and make it look exactly the way it does now, prompting her father to confide in me that "she doesn't understand yet that *home* is our family and that wherever we are is home."

I sit in a hot bath scented with rosemary oil, sipping a glass of wine in candlelight.

Trish, singer

HORIZONTAL

Kids can come up with some unexpectedly poignant thoughts. Recently Adam and Joel, my two youngest nephews, were describing the highlights of a long car trip to Cape Cod. They both were thankful they could sleep in the back seat of their parents' van.

"What's so special about that?" I inquired. (Though I had a sudden flashback to a "teenage back-seat adventure," it, of course, didn't involve sleeping!)

"When it's nighttime," Adam explained, "you can sleep in the back seat while your parents are in the front doing all the worrying."

"Yeah, they take care of everything," added Joel. "And when you wake up, you're a lot closer to home and your own bed."

Home. Your own bed. My nephews' comments brought back my own earlier childhood memories. When I was a kid, we would often visit relatives in Toronto, which meant a long trip home to Hamilton in the dark. Usually, I would have to fight my brother for leg room, but with the predictable stern threats coming from the front seat, Steven and I would settle down and eventually fall asleep. I slept so deeply, in fact, that I was never aware of being tenderly carried from the back seat all the way up to my room. Somehow, I always woke up in the safest place in the whole world—my own bed.

I also fondly recall my dad's nightly "check on the kids" ritual before he retired for the evening. Sometimes I would be dimly conscious of his tour of my room. He would tug on my blanket to cover me up, whether I needed it or not. Then he would open my window just a crack more for fresh air.

There is almost nothing better than being in your very own bed: your favourite pillow, your toasty warm feet; flannel sheets in winter, cool cotton ones in summer, a cozy blanket tucked under your chin. I love vacations, but nothing compares to that first blissful deep sleep after returning to my own bed. "I love everything about bed," effused Shelley Stein with a dreamy smile. "I love

I watch our mother cat nurture her three kittens, which has taught me many life lessons.

Louise, legal assistant

sleeping, lounging, and the warmth, comfort, and nurturing I feel in bed. Most kids hated naps, but not me. When I was four years old, I asked my mother if I could have a nap. She said, 'You're too old to have a nap.' But I insisted. I've loved naps ever since."

Think about the word "bed" for a moment, and the meaning it conveys for you. "Bed" can represent a harbour of comfort and safety, a sanctuary for a conversation or a cuddle, love, and promises, even a hideaway for our tears and fears. Too much bed can signal depression; it may act as a refuge during pain and illness. Too little bed may mean workaholism or insomnia. In bed we dream, worry, reminisce, cry, meditate, and pray; in bed we reflect on today and hope for tomorrow.

THE FLANNEL CONNECTION

As infants, we are emotionally bonded to our mothers, who love, cuddle, and care for us. As we get older—between two and six— we realize that our moms aren't there strictly for us, so we often become attached to a teddy bear, a soft blanket, or a doll. According to Dr. Paul Horton, a psychiatrist who has done extensive research on solace: "These objects remind us of our all-important first relationship and they help us make the transition from our mothers as our entire world to living in the world at large."

"It was like a part of my skin," Erica, a pretty 21-year-old patient reminisced, describing a white and blue snugly blanket with tassels that her grandmother crocheted and gave her on the day she was born. "I always wanted a little sister, so when I was six, my mom got me a kitten. I named her Polly, and used to dress her up in my blanket. Sometimes, I'd find her sleeping on my bed all curled up in it. I was always a bit shy and insecure, so when I was ten, I decided to wean myself from the blanket, and I gave it to Polly. For 13 years Polly and my snugly blanket were the two biggest holders of my tears." At that moment, Erica looked as

I talk to my guardian angels every day.

Wendy, manager

though she was going to cry. "When Polly died last week, my mom put a little pillow and sheet in a cardboard box and gave it to me. I placed Polly in the box and covered her with the old snugly blanket. My whole childhood was in that box."

Even as adults, we still need those "snugly blankets"—now called *solacing objects*—items that recapture the soul of our childhood, and that deep sense of soothing comfort we felt when we were young. I recognized my own need for solacing objects when I lived alone after my marriage ended. I noticed that when I slept on flannel sheets, I would be unconscious almost as soon as my head hit the pillow. But it wasn't just flannel that gave me solace. Likewise, foods such as mashed potatoes, peanut butter and jam, hot oatmeal with brown sugar, Campbell's tomato soup with a million crackers scrunched in, and even the occasional Kraft Dinner nurtured me in a way that dinner in a four-star restaurant could never have accomplished. I soon realized how powerful these childhood connections really are.

Solacing objects can take many forms—teddy bears, pets, music, a favourite book, photographs, and memories. David, an engineer, can easily re-create his childhood feelings. "When I was ten, my school friend Larry taught me the importance of little rewards. I would save my nickels and dimes so I could treat myself to a Dinky toy. Now I still like to reward myself by buying something small—a special tool, or maybe a CD. I get the same excitement I had back then. It's funny how the feelings don't change."

Yes, indeed, some feelings never change. Perhaps that is why we all relate so readily to "Peanuts," and to the reminders that the Charlie Brown in all of us never forgets feelings of failure and rejection, or the need to be loved and comforted. In a recent episode, Sally is on the telephone with Linus, saying, "Yes, I heard you lost the first game of the season. I've never seen my big brother so depressed. Sure, I'll tell him." In the last frame, we see Charlie Brown, forlorn and miserable, sitting on the floor, sucking his thumb, and clutching Linus's precious blanket. Sally then reassures

I tape the telephone conversations I have with my grandchildren and play them back when I want to smile.

Micki, *broadcast journalist*

him: "Linus says to keep the blanket as long as you want." We all need compassionate friends who truly understand our moments of need.

One cold January night, I was sitting in front of my computer with frozen kneecaps and a runny nose. I suddenly had a *heart-warming* solution for my cold legs. I went downstairs, opened the hall closet, and took out the mink coat that my mom had left to me eight years earlier, which I hadn't yet worn. As I placed the coat over my legs, I felt completely warmed and enveloped by her spirit. Now I use her coat all winter long to comfort me both inside and out!

I recently discovered that one of my sinus pressure techniques provided solace for a patient suffering from tension headaches. Whenever I gently massaged Robert's forehead, he sighed very deeply and then relaxed completely. When I asked him about this, he recalled that his mom always used to caress his forehead before bedtime. Robert, who realizes just how powerful that specific childhood memory is for him, now strokes his own forehead whenever he feels stressed.

No matter what our age or stage in life, we all need to create an oasis of solace in our daily life. Think about what or who has nurtured you. A flannel nightgown? A hot bubble bath? A massage? Childhood songs? Hot chocolate with marshmallows? A soft, fluffy cat? Do you have a special pillow you sleep on? Teddy bears on your bed? (I have three bears and a moose!) Think of some of your special happy childhood memories and you will rekindle that feeling of being loved and cared for. Solace may be as close as two arms giving you a hug—one of the best feelings in the whole world.

LIFE CYCLES

I cry easily, especially when I'm overjoyed or touched. I spent ten minutes in the theatre washroom splashing cold water on my

I savour every drop of my freshly squeezed orange juice in the morning.

Michael, pension fund manager

swollen red eyes after seeing the movie *Life Is Beautiful*. I weep at all family events—weddings, bar mitzvahs—don't ask me about funerals! And the older I get, the more sentimental and blubbering I become. I cried when my nephew Michael and his wife, Julie, asked me to be godmother to their newborn daughter, Tovah. At the baby-naming ceremony I carried this precious miracle on a white satin pillow and presented her to my family. The first girl in our family since I was born 50 years ago, we welcomed this baby as daughter, granddaughter, great-granddaughter, niece, and great-niece. As I wiped away the tears (then and now), I reflected on the significance of this ritual for me and every member of my family.

Rituals connect us with our past and provide continuity in the present. Ceremonies and traditions link us to future generations. Rituals are not mindless routines, as they give our life meaning, shape, and a sense of harmony and rhythm. Rituals also give families a feeling of cohesion. For a child, the simple ritual of being tucked into bed with a beloved teddy bear, singing a favourite song, or hearing the words "I love you" each night provides emotional stability and nurturing.

Barbara Rosenberg asks her eight-year-old son, Jake, the same question each night: "Why are we lucky?"

"Because we have each other," he answers.

"Rituals transform the mundane into something special," believes Wendy Cecil-Cockwell, mother of Gareth, Malcolm, and Tess. "Sadly, the ritual of giving my kids piggybacks on the way to bed is coming to an end, because they are getting too heavy. Each night that I'm able to lift Gareth is a bonus and a victory. I also say prayers with the kids. Then we repeat together, "A wonderful day is a day that you actually get to see the end of."

Rituals are the glue that binds couples together. Talking together in bed before sleeping, using pet names, and a kiss and a hug goodbye each morning are all actions that connect us to another human being. Alan Schwartz and his wife created a romantic Friday night ritual when they were first married. "By candlelight,

When I come home from work, I hug my dog and then I stand up straight and take a deep breath, which means I'm now home.
Amanda, IT director

we would get into the bath, sit facing each other, and just talk. There were no distractions. We couldn't answer the phone or change TV channels. We began to look forward to our relaxing night of solitude. Now that our two children are older, we have changed our bath ritual to a once-a-week date. We go to a quiet restaurant alone, which gives us the opportunity to be together."

Every night for the past 50 years, Dr. Robert Salter and his wife, Robina (Robbie), perform a bedtime ritual: They kneel beside their bed and pray together. "We each have our individual prayer list of about 20 people—family and friends who may be ill, or dealing with sorrow or adversity," Dr. Salter explains. "This ritual is our time to be with each other in a meaningful way. If we are away on vacation or even if I am travelling alone to speak at a conference, we still pray each night."

Often we aren't aware of how intricately rituals are woven into the fabric of a relationship. Judge Roger Conant, 77, wiped away a tear as he described his first Christmas without Fran, his much-loved wife of 52 years. "I remember the little things we shared. Fran would prepare a huge cauldron of a mixture for Christmas pudding, and each family member would give it a stir and make a wish. The preparation would involve everyone and occur over two weekends. Now our ritual of making Christmas pudding each year with the whole family means so much to me. Thankfully, one of our close friends will help me make the pudding next year so we can continue this family tradition."

Rituals give structure, meaning, and rhythm to daily life. Artist Doris McCarthy, 89, begins each day in the same way—with a celebration. "I wake up early, get out of bed, make a cup of instant coffee, and take it back to bed. I gather my loved ones [cats] and for 45 minutes I am in the moment, enjoying being there, being awake. It is my luxury to do nothing useful at this time. Then I get up, get dressed, make my bed, tidy the bathroom and bedroom, feed the cats, and do my exercises. After that, I retire to my study for quiet time—meditation and spiritual reading. When I'm finished

Every day I read and save meaningful quotes and sayings from the newspaper or from friends.

Micki, broadcast journalist

I have a damn good breakfast consisting of a Florida orange, vitamins, my own granola with half a banana sliced on top, and a piece of my homemade white bread, thinly sliced and toasted crisp, topped with my own orange marmalade. A cup of tea ends my morning ritual and then I begin to attack the day's work."

I laughed when Sylvia Molson, 80, told me about her mother's nightly ritual to make sure her nine teenagers were home safe after going out at night. "She had a roll call. As one of the kids would walk up the stairs, Mom would call out from her bed, 'Sylvia? Abe? Leonard? Esther?' and you'd have to answer. Sometimes we tried saying someone else's name, especially when we were late, but she always knew!"

My brother Steven and I have a private ritual that began in high school. I am not sure exactly when it began or even why. What matters is the constancy, predictability, and meaning behind it—just between us. In our salutations in a letter or birthday card—even in e-mail—Steven writes, "Dear Elaine (*ma soeur*)," and I write, "Dear Steven (*mon frère*)." In the overall scheme of things, this gesture is pretty small, and yet for me it speaks volumes about love, caring, and timelessness. It's only now, in the middle years of my life, that I deeply understand how much these exchanges mean to me.

Rituals need not be profound to be significant. Birthdays, holidays, graduations, and reunions are all celebrations of everyday life. Rites of passage, those things that we do for the first time that, in fact, have always been celebrated by humanity, also need to be acknowledged. Even ordinary activities—like riding a bike, driving a car, leaving home for university, or your first job—can be transformed into significant events when they are honoured with love and a sense of wonder. I invite you to explore the rituals in your life and create new ones. Family dynamics often change. Rituals can smooth transitions in relationships, particularly if there are new family members such as stepchildren or stepsiblings. Think about what is important to you at certain seasons of

Every day I try to help one patient who is down or sad to laugh.
                                              Mary Ann, *chiropractor*

the year. Dr. Salter gathers his five children and eight grand-children together to observe Thanksgiving. He says, "It is a fit-ting time to express what we are grateful for and what matters to us in life."

A GIFT OF HOPE

Mom wore a heart-shaped marcasite pin with a Star of David inset; brilliant steel-grey stones faceted to glitter like diamonds. That pin accompanied her everywhere—on coats, dresses, col-lars, and suit lapels. Next to her wedding ring, it was her favourite piece of jewellery.

One day I arrived for a visit at the nursing home and Mom opened the door without saying hello. "I've lost my pin," she lamented, looking pale and distraught. We looked everywhere—in her lingerie drawer, in the clothes closet, even in the zippered compartment of her purse, a cache for the occasional 50-dollar bill. Nothing. She never talked about the pin after that, and I never mentioned it, fearful that I might upset her. Eventually I forgot about it.

When she died, the director of the nursing home gently asked my brother and me to remove all of Mom's possessions. With a grim face, I met Steven in Mom's room holding a package of green garbage bags. We didn't say much to each other but our eyes spoke volumes. Steven took the television, a small walnut bookshelf, some dusty hardcover classics, a cardboard box filled with loose photographs, and about six photo albums. I opened the dresser drawers and scooped up enough clothing to fill the first two garbage bags. Shoes and purses filled another bag. Then I removed her dresses and blouses from the hangers, and placed them in the remaining bags. The scent of L'Air du Temps, Mom's cologne, lingered in the walls of that tiny room, and in the clothes, draw-ers, and closets. I drove back to Toronto with six full bags in my

When I drift off to sleep at night, I am always holding my wife's hand.
Stephen, banker

car, filled with the history and memories of my mother.

For over a year the bags sat untouched in the corner of a spare bedroom. And then one day it just happened. I felt ready. I began to sort her things into two piles—the Salvation Army and Dembe's Salvation. Stockings, brassieres, slips, and cardigans—the mountain for charity was growing. I held up one of her satin-sheen girdles and laughed out loud. I remembered Mom grabbing both ends of the fabric and taking a deep breath while I struggled to zip her up, careful not to pinch her skin. I sure don't need this, I thought, and threw it on top of the pile.

Mom loved to knit colourful wool slippers. Sometimes I wore mine to bed. I found a plastic bag with four new pairs and kept them. Eight pairs of worn-out shoes, stretched and misshapen from the ravages of a bunion, went to charity. I glanced down at my left foot and its identical bunion and smiled.

In the last garbage bag there were more dresses to donate. I held up one that Mom had worn often—a black and grey plaid dress with shiny steel-gray buttons. I saw something glittery camouflaged on the collar. Tears filled my eyes as I removed Mom's precious Star of David pin. I walked over to the window and held it up to the light. It was more beautiful than I had remembered.

That this unexpected gift—this small pin, no bigger than a quarter—could fill me with such joy, hope, and a sense of connection with the past, meant only one thing. My heart was at peace once more.

I wear pretty underwear every day, even when I'm pregnant.
Dorothy, director of sales

PLAYING

Rekindlegarten

Kindergarten recess has just begun,
Magical days with games and fun,
Dreams came true with make-believe,
Whatever my imagination conceived.
Tooth fairies, rainbows, a pot of gold,
Mysteries of life routinely unfold.
"Happily ever after" bedtime stories end,
Supposed to be asleep, sometimes I'd pretend.
Wearing Mom's heels and red lipstick,
Her hand on my forehead when I got sick.
Always loved animals, had dogs and cats
Never had grandparents, life's like that.
Would tell on my brother if he said a bad word.
Got his mouth washed with soap, the yells I heard!
There were things that made me mad:
I'd shout, "It's not fair!" Sometimes I'd be sad.
Hated naps, the dark, spit out lima beans,
Yucky squash, beef tongue, and sardines,
Stood beside my mom when she baked a cake,
Licked the bowl and the beaters, a mess I'd make.
A day seemed so long, time just trickled by.
Adults were so tall, the sky, miles high.
"Are we there yet?" I'd ask, travelling by car.
When you've just had a birthday, the next one's so far.
Saturday cartoons and Mickey Mouse,
Dolls, Howdy Doody. Do you wanna play house?
My parents took trips; upon their return,
"What did you bring me?" my only concern.
Spelling bees and the lead in a play.

"Going to be famous," my dad said, "someday."
Helping, sharing, obeying mother and father.
Golden Rule, Ten Commandments,
   don't fight with your brother!
Sunday night TV family ritual of fun,
   Walt Disney, Bonanza, Ed Sullivan.
I'm not really six, I'm 51, you see
And there's no one now to look after me.
Parents are gone; new children enchant.
My brother's a grandpa; I'm a great-aunt.
I know a place that's filled with joy.
Adults need to go there, don't forget your toys.
Rekindlegarten is in your heart and soul
Of memories, of process, there is no goal
Rekindlegarten adults are given new eyes
Grateful for life's wonder, the gifts and surprise.

When I was ten years old, I became an honorary member of the Mickey Mouse Club. I owned Mickey Mouse ears and a white T-shirt with my name on the front in black thread, carefully embroidered by my mom. Sitting cross-legged three inches from the TV screen, I would patiently wait for the Mouseketeer roll call: Karen, Cubby, Annette… "ELAINE!" I yelled, loud enough, I hoped, for them to hear. It was my favourite show.

Thirty-three years later, in Disneyland, on Christmas Day, I hugged a real live Mickey Mouse, squished in with about a million other "kids" all awaiting the arrival of storybook characters at the annual Disneyland Christmas parade.

My entire childhood marched by, from Alice in Wonderland to Pinnochio. The real seven-year-olds in the crowd squealed and laughed with joy, while I sobbed tears of joy mixed with regret. Regret for my lost youth, and for taking life too seriously for too long. The tears nourished me; my heart opened like a flower kissed

I try to discover something new on my daily nature walk with my dog—a tree, bird, or secret garden.
                              Dorothy, environmental specialist

by the rain. As I stood there, I remembered my childhood. Life was
very serious back then. At ten years old, I had a 64-year-old dad
and a mom with a heart condition. I didn't play much and I can't
recall ever goofing off with my parents: doing silly, fun, frivolous,
playful stuff. We did, though, play adult games like Scrabble, and
we rented a cottage at the beach. I loved our weekend family out-
ings, often hiking and exploring nature.

When I became a teenager, I still didn't play. I was too intent
on being grown-up. Then, as an adult I used to feel guilty about
non-productive activities. It was easy to stay busy with my growing chiropractic practice, a host of public-speaking engagements,
and my intensive running program. In fact, I was always in running
mode, whether I wore high heels or sneakers. When a friend suggested that I learn to relax, I remarked that I had my own brand
of meditation—"The One-Minute Meditator" designed for Type-
A personalities.

My marriage ended just before my fortieth birthday, and this crisis completely changed my attitude. I began intensive therapy.
As layers of pain peeled away, I softened. I played, sang, danced,
cried when I felt like it, meditated, laughed, wrote poems, read
children's books, and sat in silence in the sunlight. I started hanging out with Velveteen Rabbits, and with my little nephews, Joel
and Adam. I played hide 'n' seek—hiding my agendas and seek-
ing joy in the present moment.

For the first time in my life, I could enjoy an activity for the
sheer pleasure of it, without judging whether something was right
or wrong or a waste of time. I went to the zoo, spent hours in toy
shops, watched reruns of I Love Lucy, and took my nephews to
the movies. Leaving my watch at home was liberating. I stopped
worrying whether I had accomplished anything great during that
day. I learned that play can be a source of peace and rest. An
activity didn't have to be "active" to be meaningful. Sometimes I
sat alone in my garden, listening to the waterfall in my goldfish
pond or watching squirrels steal seeds from the bird feeder.

I welcome the return of "Woody" the woodpecker to my bird feeder.
Jan, director of administration

I confess that I had help during this process: In fact, I had a "play" mentor. Just as I was starting to discover my playful side, I met Sharon Newman, an acting coach and personal manager from Los Angeles who "plays" for a living. Sharon was my bunk-mate at the healing retreat centre in California. There is a profound proverb: When the student is ready, the teacher will come. And I learned a lot from her.

Sharon prepares children and adults for television and movie auditions. The kids naturally know how to be playful, spontaneous, and creative. When her adult pupils allow that childlike energy to emerge, they too become actors, and many students experience personal breakthroughs in her class. "Acting is safer for them than therapy," she says. "It's easier to play a role than to delve into your own past." She uses games and improvisation exercises that require an immediate non-judgemental response, helping imagination and ideas to flow.

One glorious afternoon, as Sharon and I sat on a rock overlooking the Pacific Ocean, she explained the meaning of play. "Most people are so busy making a living and being responsible, they forget to make time for play. We need to give ourselves permission to be silly. Though it's okay for kids to make faces in the mirror and watch Saturday morning cartoons, adults are expected to act 'their age.' Play is healing. We learn more about ourselves when we are not as intense." For those grown-ups who need frivolity, Sharon has some simple suggestions: bake a cake with children (don't forget to lick the bowl and beaters), go to a park and play on the swings, play hopscotch with kids at recess, watch a children's movie or cartoons, or read children's books—Charlotte's Web, The Secret Garden, or anything by Dr. Seuss.

Sharon continued, "Children just are. They don't judge who or what they are until we, as adults, teach them to judge." Helen Kenney, an orthodontic nurse who deals with kids daily, knows first-hand what this means. In a horrible accident a year ago, a dog bit off her nose. She still wears a bandage over the healed surgeries

Each day I think silent, loving, grateful thoughts for my children and family and I feel peaceful inside.

Barbara, human resources director

even though there is no open wound or cut. Her reason? "Our society is so concerned with appearance that adults couldn't deal with my disfigurement. Kids are open and honest. They ask, 'What did you do to your nose? Can I see it?' Or 'How come you still have a bandage on your nose? It's been a year and I'm getting my braces off.' I tell them I had a very bad cut and doctors are repairing it. 'Oh, okay.' Hurt, repair, heal. End of story. With kids you don't have to get complicated. They don't have any preconceptions. They accept who you are." Helen added, "We need to unlearn all the things we know as an adult, and become more like kids." As Picasso said, "It takes one a long time to become young."

With my new outlook, I realized that children can teach us everything we need to know about using the good dishes. Kids always have first dibs on the instruction manual that's hidden in the box they come in. That's the rule. Though once upon a time we read it from cover to cover, somehow we forgot to take the refresher course. Either we were too busy, or we thought we knew it by heart, or maybe we just assumed it wasn't that important.

Well, guess what? There's a unique school called Rekindlegarten that is now offering a program for mature students. It's guaranteed to help you release inhibitions, reconnect with your creativity and imagination, and just have fun. On graduation you'll receive a "face lift"—the corners of your mouth will form a permanent grin. The days are free-flowing but the following subjects are suggested:

1. *Play 101:* You have permission to be silly whenever you want, without specific goals or a timetable. You may choose how you enjoy yourself that day, but singing at the piano, puppet play, fingerpainting, and games are always available.
2. *How Come?* You'll rediscover the joy in the smallest things, like going barefoot or dressing up for Halloween.
3. *Pet Therapy:* Cats and dogs live in residence at

I feel joyful when I find daily love notes anywhere my loving husband of 30 years decides to hide them.

Kate, *executive assistant*

Rekindlegarten to teach us about unconditional love. Play with them at recess.

4. *Childhood Passions:* You'll reconnect with whatever childhood hobbies or activities you gave up. Pupils will be asked to bring their favourite childhood lunch; a blanket, pillow, and stuffed animal for nap time; and a photo, toy, piece of artwork, or souvenir for Show and Tell.

Okay, class. The bell is ringing. No watches are allowed. Your re-education is about to begin!

WHAT TIME IS RECESS?

When I was a kid my parents rented a cottage at Wasaga Beach, known for its groomed sandy beaches and calm water you could wade in fearlessly. The beach. Just saying those words now reminds me of those playful days when I could amuse myself for hours with a plastic shovel, pail, ball, and water wings. Adults lay out on towels or lawn chairs, enjoying the warmth of the sun on their skin. It was a great family place where you could just relax and watch the waves, the clouds in the sky, or boats, endlessly. I never felt rushed at the beach; time was of no consequence. We simply got up in the morning, had breakfast, and went to the beach for the day. That was my summer and I never tired of it. Each day presented an opportunity to build something creative in the sand, learn a new swimming manoeuvre, roughhouse with my cousins, or enjoy a wonderful homemade sandwich. At the beach we were all kids—children and adults alike.

Though the beach hasn't changed over the years, the attitudes of many of the adults who go there have. They are still chilling out, far enough away from home and office to disconnect somewhat from chores and projects. Yet, despite the appearance of play, I often see evidence to the contrary. A plethora of cellphones—

When my daughter wakes up, we play the spider-tickle game, laughing joyfully together.

Terie, salesperson

checking voicemail, perhaps? And laptop computers—"just have to finish this piece for Monday's meeting!" There seems to be ambivalence about the notion of play. Perhaps people feel guilty for taking time off, or have forgotten how to play altogether. For some, playing is a reminder of those awful moments in childhood when they were picked last for the team, or told they were too short or too fat for the game. "We still play," observes anthropologist Garry Chick, Ph.D., "but much of it lacks a playful quality. Playfulness has been replaced by aggressiveness and the feeling that more needs to be crammed into less time." Witness the numbers who "work out" with the same intensity they "work in" the office.

The value of play is being studied seriously and scientifically. Play, it turns out, is not a waste of time. It reduces our stress level, restores our optimism, refreshes our spirits, and stimulates our creativity. Evidence is mounting that those who play regularly live longer and are happier. Play is getting so trendy that a work ethic that requires getting by on four hours of sleep is being replaced by the newest status symbol—enjoying a full night's sleep. And how we play varies. For a few of my athletic friends, play is physical—a rock-climbing session in a gym or bike riding through the woods. My boyfriend, Bernie, loves the strategy of playing chess. Playing for me is a game of Scrabble. Some of us get to play in our work. *The Leave It to Beaver* generation that forgot to take recess with them when they grew up should meet John Borda, 56, a "recess expert," kindergarten teacher, and all-round big kid who gave me an update on recess and a lesson on play.

"Recess hasn't changed a bit. Kids are still shooting marbles, skipping, playing hopscotch and basketball, flipping and trading cards." John feels privileged to surround himself with children who are just beginning to appreciate the joy of life. "I've learned to enjoy the here and now. When a child rushes up to me full of excitement and says, 'Look, Mr. Borda! Watch what I can do!' I have to be present and open. I focus on their discovery and share it with them. I've become a better listener, especially with family

On rainy days, I get into a hot bubble bath with a good book.
Rhoda, executive assistant

and friends. Even the most trivial events that children share with me are important in their minds. I have to give them my full attention and listen. The kids bring out my silly side. I can be goofy, spontaneous, and imaginative, and this has made me more relaxed. If I do feel grumpy for any reason, five minutes of laughing and playing with the kids will pull me out of it." John has good advice for his peers: "Adults need to remember that play has no end goal or purpose. It's not about accomplishing anything; play just *is*. Do it because it makes you feel good. Play keeps you anchored in today so that you'll be happy in the *now*."

Candice Sheldon would fit right in as the oldest kid in John's kindergarten class. At 34, this marketing consultant sings songs from her childhood every day. You might want to join her in "Itsy-Bitsy Spider" or "Twinkle, Twinkle Little Star," two of her favourites. "Singing is simple and honest and that allows me to be playful," she says. Recently, after a full day of networking and faxing and telephoning clients, she rented *Winnie the Pooh*. "Over time many adults lose that childlike instinct," she believes. "I gather up all the joy from my childhood and take it with me every day!"

"Arctic" Joe Womersley, though 74, may just be too young for kindergarten. One January morning after Toronto had experienced its biggest snowfall in memory, this runner looked out his ninth-floor apartment window and suddenly had a fun idea. "The main streets were deserted. Nothing was moving." Joe bundled up, put on his running shoes, and headed out the door. "I waded through side streets of waist-high snow, got to the main intersection, and ran five miles straight down the centre of 'busy' St. Clair Avenue. I didn't see a soul or hear a thing except for the sound of my own breathing." Joe's footprints were the only marks on the unblemished snow as he passed giant whipped-cream blobs where cars were buried. "I felt a childlike sense of wonder, almost as if I was the only person left on the planet!"

It is also a sense of wonder for which Hope Sealy, 62, is so

Each morning I step outside and soak in the smell, sight, and feel of the day—trees, flowers, sun, and sky.

Pat, executive assistant

grateful. "Life for me is a wonder. I wake up in the morning without effort. That is a wonder. I look around my bedroom and realize it's still here. I find that is a wonder. When I put on a CD, I say wow at the whole chain of events that allows me to listen to Schubert's music—from his mind, through technology, all the way to my ears. I think it's sad that many people are not aware of life's daily tiny miracles—the things we take for granted." Hope added, "I'm even conscious of the air and the fact that we breathe in and out to live. That's fantastic!"

Hope's ability to appreciate life's "wonder-filled" moments is truly a gift, and something children innately understand. Joe Thompson, an elementary school teacher for 34 years, has also learned valuable life lessons from children. "When you're a kid, there's no such thing as worry. Things will take care of themselves. Just like an Indiana Jones movie, the hero may be in peril, you don't know how he is going to get out of it, but he does. That's the confidence that kids have. If there is one thing I've learned from children, it is this: No matter what the circumstances are, you're going to make it to the other side."

CHILDREN WITH FUR COATS

Children and pets have much in common. They both exhibit the same exuberance for life, boundless energy, and spontaneity. Pets teach us how to use the good dishes. With the thump of a tail, they shift from a meditative peaceful state into blissful overdrive. Have you ever known a dog who was waiting to be happy? A dog or a cat would never think, "I really would like to see some can-opener action, then maybe a hug and some kisses, but Elaine looks busy so I'll wait 'til bedtime." Animals, full of honesty and openness, put their feelings on display, asking for what they want with no fear of rejection. And no matter what kind of day we have had, all is forgotten as they envelop us in their joy and happiness. When

I get up each morning and say a silent thank you to the universe that I am here.

Nancy, sales administrator

we return their affection, we are truly living in the moment.

We all have a basic need to love and nurture. Pets allow us to express our love and affection without fear of rejection or judgement. In return for a pat on the head, a tickle under the chin, and some food and water, pets give us complete devotion and a constant love that is unmatched in human relationships. Can you recall ever receiving the kind of frenzied, tail-thumping, whimpering, licking, jumping, running-around-in-circles euphoria that you get from a puppy in your personal relationships? A cat will give you three or four very vocal meows followed by a total body flop, paws up: That's body language for "rub my tummy."

In the reception area of your local veterinarian's office you will observe an interesting phenomenon. Almost without exception, every pet owner (including me) reveals a split personality with two distinct voices, one reserved for human contact ("I've brought Coco and Chanel in to see Dr. Weintrop") and the other a form of high-pitched baby talk. The human-pet bond invites us to express our pure selves without having to defend our feelings or actions. Such a relationship involves reciprocal, unconditional love; you and your pet bond through devotion and total acceptance. I also think that people are friendlier to each other in a vet's waiting room.

Though I wouldn't dream of trying to change my cats, we often try to change the people closest to us. On more than one occasion pet owners have confided that they like animals better than people. Perhaps this is because many individuals have interpersonal relationships that are charged with ambivalence and negative emotions. Human love and attention may be earned only with difficulty and sacrifice, or it may be entirely unavailable. But pets are an unfailing source of comfort and companionship that gives great meaning to our lives. Veterinarian Dr. Ruth Weintrop recalls, "A client agreed to have her ill cat put to sleep. Distraught and grief-stricken, she told me she could never get another animal, because after 15 wonderful years, the pain, suffering, and loss was

I compliment other women in a sincere way. It makes us both feel good.

Joan, agent

too great. When I met the same woman on the street a year later, her husband had died and she was remarrying within six months!"

Pets enrich our lives in many ways. For a child from a troubled home, a pet can be a best friend. One of my patients, now 45, shared this story with me: "I was given a wonderful cocker spaniel when I was two. That dog and I were inseparable. Seven years later, my parents divorced. My two older brothers were away at school and I was alone with my mother, who had unfortunately become an alcoholic. My dog was the only one I could talk to. He was someone I could cry to. I never had to explain myself to him; he would look at me with his big caring eyes that seemed to understand what I was feeling. He really got me through some rough times."

When I asked some of my patients the question, "What small thing do you do on a regular basis that brings joy to your life?" several immediately thought of daily pet rituals, or games. One claimed to enjoy her cat's relentless feed-me-now, meowing wake-up call, another his dog's grab-this sock-from-my-mouth tug-of-war. Pat, an advertising executive, meditates with her cat Shelley purring dreamily in her lap, sharing the experience.

As a chiropractor, I am very conscious of the healing power of touch. When we touch and caress our pets, their pleasure enriches us emotionally. Many people suffering from human touch deprivation find in their pets an unbridled outlet for their love and affection.

Consider this simple definition of happiness: "Happiness is something to do, something to look forward to, and something to love." The "something to love" can be an animal. For the many people, young and old, who live alone, pets can be companions and confidantes. We can open up completely to our pets, sharing our stories with them. And the best part? They'll never tell our secrets!

I feel the warmth of the sun on my body.

Helen, banker

Love

Your eyes speak volumes.
Soft, adoring, as I approach you,
I know what you want.
I hold you in my arms, warm bodies connecting.
So much unspoken between us, yet we understand each other.
Our love bonded and sealed from the beginning.
You: ever constant, dependable, predictable, stubborn;
Me: never wanted to change you, you were real,
always there for me.
You taught me to love unconditionally,
So easy to share with, your eyes never left mine,
I opened my heart to you.
You left me often, but I could accept that about you.
There was never anyone else, for loyalty was your watchword.
I learned never to ask where you were going.
You needed to explore the world beyond my doorstep.
You always returned, eager to see me,
hungry for my affection and touch.
I always knew what you wanted, and I gave it to you,
no questions asked.
Clean kitty litter, beef and liver stew with crunchies on top.

CHILDHOOD ON A BUN

Strictly for the sake of scientific research, I ate three jumbo kosher-style all-beef hot dogs (no buns) for dinner tonight. They were dressed with a concoction of sticky honey mustard and gourmet relish, plus all of the plain old ketchup that gushed out after one hard slap on the bottom of the bottle. My laboratory results? Dee-lish-us!

Why, you may ask, am I studying hot-dogology? Well, when a

I sit on top of a hill near my home and admire the view.
John, salesperson

patient of mine, Sule Gjoca, told me that everything he needed to know about life he learned as a hot dog vendor, I was intrigued. Sule said that it didn't take long to realize that he wasn't just selling hot dogs on a bun; he was treating adults to a taste of their childhood. Just as we tend to link popcorn with the movies, we connect hot dogs with memories of baseball games, the circus, family picnics, camping, the Santa Claus parade—anything we did as kids that was fun. Hot dogs = fun! And Sule sells fun!

Sule's hot dog cart, strategically located on a busy downtown corner, attracts a potpourri of customers, from kids, to business suits, to the homeless. "Where else but at my cart could a banker, a courier, and a bag lady eat lunch together?" he observed. "People of different backgrounds mingle together. I remember an incident where a guy pulled up in a Mercedes convertible, hops out and pays for a dog and a drink with a 50-dollar bill. Then this rough-looking, unshaven character saunters up and asks for something to eat. Without hesitation, the rich guy buys him lunch and the two of them are standing there together, eating and making small talk about life. For five minutes they were just people— two guys enjoying hot dogs on a summer day."

If you're fed up with the measly 50-minute hour at the shrink's office, park yourself in front of Dr. Sule's cart. For a couple of bucks, you can chew on a dog as well as his ear. And he'll never tell you that your time is up. "I build relationships with my regulars. Often they feel safe enough to open up and tell me their problems—financial, stress at work—even their sex life! Sometimes a few people will get into a heated discussion about politics or last night's hockey game. The hot dog stand is an open forum where everyone feels free to express their opinions."

And Sule has an eye for detail. "I bet you don't know how many different ways people dress their dogs." He wasn't referring to jewelled collars on poodles either. Before I could guess, Sule answered. "Some methodically make squiggles or straight lines, even criss-cross patterns with the mustard, relish, ketchup, and

I sit in front of the fireplace on cold winter nights.

Marty, accountant

mayo. Then there are those who decorate the bun first, without the dog in it. Many customers like onions, but they always put them on last. They stick better to the condiments and won't fall off. Some want the works—hot peppers, pickles, and cheese!" Wow! I hadn't realized that condiments can actually make a fashion statement.

Sule loves serving the young customers who can barely see over the cart. "Kids prefer a steamed or boiled dog on a non-toasted bun, either plain or maybe with just ketchup." Sometimes he'll surprise them by treating them to a bag of chips or a chocolate bar. "It's worth it just to see their wide-eyed, astonished appreciation. They can hardly believe I'm giving it to them for free!"

One day Sule noticed two Girl Guides selling cookies for their annual drive near his cart. He suggested that they come by at the end of their day and buy a hot dog. Many hours later the girls appeared—tired, hungry and carrying half a dozen unsold boxes. "Business a bit slow?" Sule inquired. They nodded. Sule reached into his cash box and bought all of the remaining cookies! Overwhelmed by his generosity, the girls eagerly paid for two hot dogs and drinks. Sule had made their day!

So the next time you are downtown craving some fun, line up at Sule's cart. You can't miss him: He's the big-bellied (too many hot dogs!) friendly-looking guy making a difference to kids—young and old. And I'll be right behind you, checking you out. Are you a "criss-cross-dresser," a "straight," or a "squiggler"?

ONCE MORE WITH FEELING

I was a lucky little girl. When I was seven, my parents introduced me to the arts via tap, ballet, and jazz dancing lessons (I dropped out—not very coordinated). Then came piano (I never practised), singing (hated the scales), and even square dancing (with my brother!). What, then, was I absolutely passionate about?

I look at the sky and notice cloud patterns.

Sharon, psychologist

Speech arts, diction, and public speaking at the Hamilton Conservatory of Music. I couldn't wait to get to my lessons, and never had to be nagged to practise. I won public-speaking contests for my school. I always got a part in whatever play our high school was producing. I had a sense quite early that I belonged on the stage, performing.

Then came university, leaving me with no time or interest for anything other than books and boys. Many years passed with little thought to childhood passions until a patient asked if I would be interested in speaking to her company on health and wellness. "What fun!" I thought, and that really rekindled my love for performing.

Have you ever been lost in the woods and walked for what seemed like miles, only to find that you were still very close to where you started? Life is a lot like that; it takes us on a convoluted path that often circles back to our beginnings. Think about the things that you loved learning as a child or a teenager. Remember home economics class and attempting to sew your first dress? Learning to play chess? Clarinet lessons? Auto mechanics or art classes? Tapping into the activities that we used to love can be fun, playful, and healing the second time around.

Christine, 53, has recently rediscovered a love of piano lessons. After a hiatus of 35 years, she purchased her first new piano. "I always had a second-hand old clunker in the house that I never played much," she said. "Now I've had six lessons from a friend. I find myself reverting back to my childhood by saying things like, 'But I played it better at home!' It's funny how the years disappear and you behave like a kid again. On the way home, I have expectations that I'll do better next time. It seems that the need for approval, for praise, for someone to say, 'That's good—let's move on to the next piece,' never leaves us no matter how old we are. I get a real sense of accomplishment. You don't have to have talent. It's just fun picking up the threads of something you loved to do."

I make a big pot of healthy soup every Sunday to last the whole week.
Pat, marketing

"The only time I sang as a child was at the Sabbath table," recalls Bernie Klein, 62. "I've since developed a great love for music, so I decided a year ago to take singing lessons. The teacher is very supportive, so I don't feel badly breathing incorrectly or singing off key. After an hour of singing, I feel carefree, loose. I sing everywhere, even in the car. It's a wonderful sense of freedom—like being a kid again!"

Reading was a childhood passion for Dr. Marie Murphy, and as a parent she loved to read to her children. Now 80, she volunteers her time reading to the blind once a week and to kids three times per week as part of a storytelling group. "I get a transfusion of energy when I read to kids," Marie says. "They're wide-eyed and open-mouthed." She still finds time to read to her grown children and young grandchildren. "It's pure joy when Mom reads to me just as she did when I was small," says Irene Wright, 40.

Reflect on the hobbies, sports, leisure, and creative activities that you loved to do. What did you give up when life got in the way? What have you been promising to do "one of these days" or "when I have more time"? What talents and gifts have you buried or abandoned because you're not a kid any more? When you were a child, what did you dream of becoming when you grew up? Go back to what you loved to do! When you start retrieving memories and fragments of your childhood passions, a door will open to Rekindlegarten. Inside you'll find a world where anything is possible—you just have to try it!

FUNNY BONES

It's Friday night, a sweaty summer evening in the city, and I am standing in the middle of one of Toronto's busiest intersections with about 30,000 other damp bodies. No, this is not a peace protest or the Gay Pride parade. We are all waiting for the start of a giant street festival. A huge stage is set up in the middle of the

I choose a slightly different route on my morning walk to look at neighbours' gardens.

Liz, entrepreneur

road, and a well-known comic strolls out to warm up the crowd. With a straight face and sombre voice he begins, "I want you to look all around at the people standing beside you and behind you. Just think. None of you got invited to a cottage this weekend!" A roar of laughter ripples through the crowd. The party has officially begun!

Subtle humour is the best—those unexpected, simple, precise observations of life. The crowd at the festival laughed over our shared experience—stuck at home in the summer. We laughed at what we knew to be true. A "Seinfeld" commentary on life reaches out like a playful finger and tickles our funny bones. Here's a sample: "Have you ever noticed when you're a kid the whole world is *up*? As in, I want to be a grown-*up*, or wait *up*, or can I stay *up*?' For parents, the world is *down*. As in, slow *down*, sit *down*, put that *down*!"

But it's more than just our bones that get a workout when we laugh. Scientific studies confirm that laughter is healthy not only for our emotions, it also accelerates healing by stimulating the immune system. A good chuckle promotes the activity of natural "killer cells," which are crucial to battling and preventing disease. Humour also helps us to cope with whatever challenges we are facing in life, and acts as a catalyst to allow us to move through loss or grief.

One rarely laughs during a funeral, unless you are Billy Crystal playing the role of Buddy the comedian in the poignant film *Mr. Saturday Night*. He begins the eulogy for his deceased mother with a serious face: "When my brother told me that Mom had passed away, the first thing I said to him was, 'Did you get her recipe for kugel?' Mom loved to cook; until I was 16 I thought my name was 'Here, taste this.'" Well, everyone at the funeral and in the movie audience roared with laughter.

We now know how crucial the mind-body connection is for healing. Our thoughts, feelings, and emotions communicate with every cell in our body. So when Queen Elizabeth Hospital, a

My husband and I both work shifts, so we go out on a breakfast date once a week.

Janet, customer service representative

chronic care hospital and rehabilitation centre in Toronto, opened their Laughter Lounge in 1992, there was great interest in the program. The hospital created a large comfortable room equipped with Charlie Chaplin movies, *I Love Lucy* videos, funny books, and cartoons. In this special place, patients swallow laughter, the best medicine, and give their internal organs a solid workout. Erika Arndt, manager of the social work department at the hospital, believes that laughter is a springboard to recovery. "Some patients can't speak in the first stages following a stroke, but a smile can signal some progress," she says. "This room is a licence to be silly, which helps staff, patients, and their families deal with issues of loss and grief."

Earl Crangle has a special understanding of how humour can help us deal with grief. In 1965 Earl was sitting beside his father-in-law in the back seat of a stretch limousine, on their way to the funeral of Earl's 27-year-old wife, who had died suddenly from an undiagnosed disease. "We couldn't speak," he recalled. "With complete mournful silence we both sat there numb, staring straight ahead." As the car moved forward, Earl looked for something to focus on. He attempted to see the back of the limousine driver's head, but it wasn't visible. "All I could see was the back of the seat. I said to my father-in-law, 'I don't think anyone is driving this car.'" Earl leaned forward to take a better look. "There was the driver, all four feet, six inches of him. His head didn't reach above the seat. I told my father-in-law and we both burst out laughing. The spell of unbearable grief was broken and we were able to face that painful day. I realized then that the healing process can begin through humour, even at the lowest ebb. I knew then I would be able to go on with my life."

My brother Steven, 53, loves to laugh and goof around with his favourite buddy, Allen, his best friend since grade nine. Allen and Steven share a playful camaraderie that has endured 35 years of life experience—from high school loves and losses to marriage, kids, divorce, and the loss of parents. Over the years they have

I try to teach my young children something new about life each day.
Dedena, customer service

concocted a golf "ritual" that is triggered only when the score is close. They try deliberately to throw each other's game off. Just as one is about to hit the ball, Steven or Allen will yell out a certain girl's name, reviving memories of disastrous high school romances or some other embarrassing incident. Both players are regularly reduced to hysterical laughter, and the golf game is inevitably declared "unofficial." I don't know which is the more beneficial exercise—the golf or the uproarious laughter!

Sometimes an unexpected laugh can diffuse a volatile situation. The following incident from my childhood still makes me smile. The disciplinary "tool" in our home was the *dreaded fly swatter*. After one typical and noisy brother-sister fight, I could hear my mother's angry voice and quick footsteps as she marched down the hall, weapon in hand. As she was about to give Steven a whack, the rubber end of the fly swatter flew off and sailed across the room. Mom, Steven, and I broke into fits of laughter and the fight was forgotten. Saved by a chuckle!

Twenty-four hours after news of Bill Clinton's sexual dalliances hit the airwaves, jokes surfaced by the dozen across North America. Anyone who ever dreamed of telling a joke with a guaranteed laugh had one-liners free for the picking. And jokes that are (ahem) lewd can serve as instant icebreakers at stuffy social gatherings. During the first frenzied week of the "Clinton commotion," I attended a wedding reception. I was in an evening gown, faking my best manners and being introduced to several elegant-looking couples. One man in the group immediately began telling Clinton oral sex jokes! Sure beats the predictable: "So, how do you know the bride and groom?"

So for all you serious people who think you may be missing a laughter gene, remember the last line in my poem "Use the Good Dishes": "When you live, *laugh*, and love, the good dishes on the table of life you have set." We are totally present when we experience laughter, that life-enhancing, healing, relaxing, all-natural prescription for stress.

I love the aroma of freshly ground coffee beans and the delicious cup of coffee I make in the morning.

                                                                    Richard, consultant

HOW COME?

They were so mesmerized with the magician they didn't notice me, but I couldn't take my eyes off of them. Two children sat on their father's lap, wide-eyed, bouncing, giggling, and squealing with delight. They sat next to me, spellbound, while Lance Burton, grand illusionist, put on his spectacular show. Why, I wondered, glancing around at the subdued adults in the audience, do we lose this innocent freshness, this capacity for wonder, amazement, and *joy*?

For a child, life is one big surprise party, planned just for them. Their curiosity knows no boundaries. How come worms come out on the sidewalk after the rain? How come birds don't get cold in the winter? How come the sky is blue? While an adult is oblivious, a child will walk down the street and notice a hairy caterpillar, an orange-winged butterfly, and an elephant-shaped cloud. "Kids are enchanted by the smallest, most trivial things," acknowledges Robert Munsch. "If I visit a new town, I avoid tours given by adults—they'll show me the boring post office. But a tour given by kids is a treat—'Here is where we throw rocks in the river, here is the neatest tree for climbing, here is the best hill for tobogganing.' Childhood is so magical." Unfortunately, kids are in a big hurry to grow up.

For adults, the awareness of the passing of time sometimes casts a pall over a pleasurable moment or event, while children inhabit a world where enjoyment is not burdened with thoughts of "next" or "this won't last." Last summer, I was completely riveted by the spectacular finals of a fireworks competition, which was synchronized to classical music. It was disheartening to hear an adult nearby announcing intermittently to his children how much time was left until the show's end. Another time, while on vacation, my girlfriend was already organizing limousine service for the return flight home—five minutes after we had checked into our tropical island hotel. I think we all need to write the following

I love the feeling of snuggling up with my two boys, aged four and two, when they crawl into my bed to wake me up.
                                        Paddy, small business owner

words on a Post-it note for our fridge door: "Yesterday's the past, tomorrow's the future, but *today* is a gift. That's why it's called the *present!*"

How can we regularly give ourselves gifts of wonder and curiosity when it's easy to become stale and bored with the predictable and familiar? How do we get excited again over the reliable return of the tulips and daffodils in spring? One way is through the power of memory. You can start by digging out your dusty childhood photographs. That was *you* in those photos! Remember some silly childhood events that you loved. It's not as if we can't still behave like children. "I had a ball building a dream dollhouse for Ryan, my three-year-old granddaughter," says big kid and grandfather David Talbot. It took him over a hundred hours to cut, sand, paint, and assemble this labour of love, a three-storey Bayberry cottage complete with windows, staircase, and roof gables. "I get so much pleasure out of playing pretend with her and that magical dollhouse. If I had known that grandchildren were so much fun, I would have skipped having children and started with them!"

As David understands, given the right toy, everyone can become a child again. So buy yourself a teddy bear or a Monopoly set. Spend a few hours reading the Hardy Boys adventure books. Make a list of five hobbies that sound like fun and commit yourself to trying two of them. Make a list of five outrageous places that you have never visited and commit to exploring one of them. Make a list of the five silliest things you would like to try once in a lifetime and then do them all! Dress up for Halloween. Explore. Play baseball. Go barefoot. Get dirty. Use the fancy soap. Eat chocolate chip cookies while they're still warm. Buy popsicles. Play croquet. Dance outside in the rain. Make up a reason to have a party. Create your own personal birthday and Valentine's Day cards.

I asked Robert Munsch, the famous children's author and storyteller, how he would teach adults to be more playful. "When you wake up in the morning, start your day with the question, 'What am I going to enjoy today?' This puts an emphasis on being

I try to give my time and energy to help someone each day.
Nancy, financial planner

open to an adventure or on having fun, rather than on a worry or on making money. I meet many adults who are unhappy with their lives, and they can be so serious. Life is only as interesting as you make it! I regularly travel by limousine from Guelph to the Toronto airport. When I get in and say, 'Where's everybody going?' everyone talks to one another. Otherwise it's dead silence the whole way."

Finally, make a personalized note to stick on your bathroom mirror, office computer, or car dashboard that says, What am I going to enjoy today? When you take this question to heart, you will automatically be enrolled in Rekindlegarten, a warm place filled with play, laughter, and joy.

P.S. If you stay clean, you'll never have fun! — Joey, age 10

KEEPING THE FANTASY

One afternoon when I was visiting my uncle George at his condominium, there was a crowd in the lobby. People were enjoying a huge Christmas display—a miniature village complete with a castle with four huge turrets. There were dozens of characters in period costume strolling through town, three electric trains, a streetcar, and even a skating rink with skaters. I studied each section with the other spellbound adults and children, trying not to miss one tiny piece of the fantasy. In one corner was a little red schoolhouse, horse and buggy carriages, a book shop, bank, and town hall. There was even a church with stained glass windows and a synagogue with a gold dome! One of the trains, with "Denver South Park" and "Pacific Railroad" painted on its side, pulled tiny rocking horses. The trains disappeared through a tunnel in a mountain. My eyes found Alice in Wonderland partying at the Mad Hatter's tea party, and even the Cheshire Cat was invited, along with several rabbits. I glanced at an older gentleman beside me whose eyes sparkled with delight as he

Every Sunday at the same time, my best friend and I visit each other by telephone.

Hannah, librarian

inched his way closer for a better view. I asked why he thought people loved this exhibit so much. "It is so far away from Monday realism," he replied. "This scene takes us back to a time when imagination had a more important part in our thinking. Certainly, it reminds me of my childhood." He laughed and said, "I'm one of the last to admit that Santa Claus doesn't exist. Down deep, adults do have the ability to appreciate the magic in life. This display brings it to the surface."

I became preoccupied with finding out who had created this display and it didn't take me long to locate him. Ralph Farrell, 72, was trained as an architectural technologist and interior designer. Twenty years ago for a company Christmas party, the employees made a small display with Christmas trees fashioned out of wire, a mountain with a ski lift, and dolls with crocheted hats and skirts. They added an electric train and cut a tunnel through the mountain. Five years later, Ralph, who had shown a keen interest in expanding the display, inherited the project. Like most creative endeavours, the little project grew! "This has been a 15-year labour of love," he admitted. "Every night I go to sleep thinking about some little thing I can add or improve on." The platform that holds the display is now forty-three feet long. According to Ralph's estimate, approximately 300 characters come alive in the scene. It took him six months just to build the synagogue with the gold dome. I asked him why he works so hard on the display. "This is a gift for others," he replied softly. "My pleasure comes from seeing the joy it brings—especially to the children. I grew up during the Depression and never had an electric train. So this is special for me too. We need to keep the fantasy in life, especially at our age!"

THE ENCHANTED WINDOW

For 11 years I've been looking out my office window, located on the third floor of a four-storey red-brick medical building. I've

Every night I recite a prayer for married couples to keep my relationship with my husband vibrant.

Marilee, teacher

angled my treatment table so that I can clearly absorb the view while I palpate, massage, and manipulate patients. The scene is always the same. Each day brings a caravan of mothers and nannies to the park, with children eager to play on the swings, slides, and rocking horses. This is Peter Pan Park, a green patch of heaven in the city, framed by giant old oak trees with low branches begging to be climbed.

On this particular day, all four swings are occupied, children's legs pointing to the sky to seek momentum. A toddler supported by two strong female arms rocks gleefully on a red horse attached to a blue spring. Two little girls with plastic shovels and pails crouch over a mound of sand. A mom waits at the bottom of the slide while her son readies himself at the top.

It may seem unfathomable that this window could possibly be a gift for my spirit. But every day it serves as a reminder to be playful. I am witness to the timelessness of life. Forty-five years ago this "grown-up" was that laughing child. There will always be children playing in this park to remind us that the simple things in life—a ball, bird, or tree—can spark curiosity, adventure, laughter, and delight. Children teach me to notice and appreciate little things—that the days are getting longer, the smell in the air after the rain, a woodpecker tapping on bark. There is a low-lying oak branch so close to my window that I can see buds forming on it in early spring. I still feel a wide-eyed excitement no matter how many times I witness the unfolding of the seasons.

Peter Pan Park, so aptly named, rekindles memories of the Mary Martin musical. "Never growing up" sounds idyllic; however, we need to and must grow up into mature, responsible, and loving human beings. I do not want to overidealize childhood; I certainly wouldn't want to relive mine. But how much more joyful would our lives be if we held on to those childlike qualities of wonder, enthusiasm, and playfulness? Spend time with children; borrow them if you don't have any of your own to play with. Volunteer at a children's hospital or at a kids' camp. Find ways to

Once a week I choose a drawer in my house to clean and reorganize.
Louise, salesperson

inject play into your work. Dr. Janet Tamo dresses up as the tooth fairy (complete with halo and giant toothbrush) every Halloween in her dental office. "You've been a very special patient today," she will say to children, who are then allowed to choose one or two items from her special toy box filled with yo-yos, wall-walkers, friendship bracelets, and gum (dentist-approved).

We all have an enchanted window to look out of every day— if not in reality, at least in our hearts and minds. To look at life through a child's eyes, we must choose to change the depth of our vision. Rekindlegarten will give you new eyes.

My husband and I give each other massages with scented oil.
                                                          Mary, *designer*

EXPLORING

The Boogeyman

No one has ever seen him, but we knew he was around.
No point in ever searching, he'll never be found.
This scary man appears when it's dark at night,
Under the bed or in a closet, instilling fear and fright.

Never doubted my brother when he warned me to beware
Of the boogeyman in the cellar. I never went there, I swear.
Forget the third-floor attic or anywhere he might have been,
This boogeyman is the scariest thing that I have *never* seen.

Sometimes tucked in bed, I thought that I could hear
A tapping sound like footsteps. Is he lurking near?
I hold my breath in fear, heart full of palpitations,
Parents try to reassure me, "It's only your imagination."

Should I take a chance and risk crawling out of bed?
I have to go to the bathroom, I'd rather hold it in instead.
I'll never make it to morning, but I'll run as fast as I can.
I pray I won't bump into the invisible boogeyman.

Whenever it is dark and you think you're all alone.
For sure that's when he'll come, but from where is unknown.
Maybe when you're bad, parents ask him to appear,
I promise I'll be good, each day and every year.
Now that I'm an adult and think back on childhood fears,
We never get rid of the boogeyman, no matter what our years.
For there's always something deep inside we're afraid of, and yet
The kid in our heart remembers what grown-ups try to forget.

EVERYDAY COURAGE

Four years ago, while getting ready for bed, an animal story near the end of the news caught my attention. Scarlett, a white, scraggly stray cat, was found saving her four-week-old kittens from a fire in her home, an abandoned garage, in Brooklyn, New York. She traded in at least eight of her nine lives returning to the burning building to carry each of her five loved ones to safety. The firefighter who discovered her, burned and almost blinded, was amazed as Scarlett tapped her chin on each of the kitten's singed heads to be sure all had been rescued. Apparently I was not the only one touched and inspired by her courage. While Scarlett and her brood recovered in an animal hospital, over 6000 offers for adoption poured in from all over the country.

There is a Scarlett in every one of us. Although she was driven by instinct, given similar circumstances we would likely have acted in the same way. Courage would replace any momentary fear. We would have done what was necessary. We are reminded that ordinary human beings, like this common feline, possess the strength to do extraordinary things.

Though courage is a part of our everyday lives, few people admit to being courageous, believing it to be associated mainly with exceptional risks and heroic deeds. It takes courage to express our true feelings, to believe in our ideas, or to face what we fear. It is an act of courage to take risks, to say no, to make changes in our life—big and small. When faced with pain and adversity, just getting out of bed in the morning may be courageous. We demonstrate the courage to persevere after the loss of loved ones.

Courage plays a role in everything we do, even when we aren't conscious of it. Living alone after a divorce, starting a new career, asking your boss for a raise, even speaking to a stranger in an elevator requires a measure of courage. Courage teaches us to grow, learn, and stretch beyond our boundaries as we deal with life's challenges.

At the end of the day, I play my organ for 45 minutes while drinking a couple of beers.

Peter, manager

Reesa Kassirer, a marriage therapist for over 30 years, counsels individuals and couples struggling with personal and family issues. "Facing yourself takes courage," she feels. "I have the greatest admiration for those who can follow through and stay with counselling. It takes courage, tenacity, and will. Many people are fearful about what they will discover about themselves."

And the most rewarding part of courageously taking that first step? "You own your stuff, then continue on your journey, feeling free and considerably lighter. Less baggage!" Reesa replied.

Artist Helen McLean, now 72, displayed remarkable courage when she decided at 50 to live by herself for a year to pursue her passion. "I was an artist pretending to be a housewife, and I knew I had to stop postponing my dreams. I just didn't want to give any more dinner parties." That autumn, Helen left her family and moved to a small town to spend all of her time painting. "Initially, I was lonely beyond words, but by spring I knew what direction my life would take from then on." After a year Helen returned home with enough work for her first solo art exhibition. She has been following this creative path ever since.

Stephen Burns would not call himself courageous, and yet that is exactly how I would describe this charismatic 57-year-old accountant and keen sailor. An admitted risk-taker, he initially panicked when asked to take over the helm of the Starlight Children's Foundation, an organization he has been involved with since the loss of his daughter, Stephanie. "I thought, 'What do I know about running anything? There's marketing, bills. How could I possibly run the whole show?'" Then courage crept in through the back door. "I looked into my heart and knew I had to do it. The things that scare you are always the best things to do." Stephen understands that the demons we fear are often worse in our imagination than in reality. Courage levels the mountains we produce in our minds. He told a story about a sailing friend who invited him to crew on his boat, which was crossing the Atlantic in the fall. Steve immediately accepted. "I told him, 'I've always

I love seeing joy on the faces of new moms after they've given birth.
Wendy, nurse

dreamed of crossing the Atlantic in a sailboat. You're on!'" With four months until their departure to mull it over, fears began to dance in Stephen's mind. "What if there are sea serpents, or pirates? Maybe the crew won't like me and they'll throw me overboard!" Again, courage prevailed. "I realized that I had to go. Not only had I made a commitment to my friend, I knew that when you meet your fear, it doesn't matter: win or lose, it's the biggest victory in the world. Just taking something on is enough to feel good about yourself." The sailing trip, as it turned out, was uneventful. "I didn't even see a big wave!"

RISKY BUSINESS

As the chiropractor for the Hummingbird Centre for the Performing Arts in Toronto, I am regularly called on to dekink the muscles and joints of visiting performers—actors, dancers, and singers. So it was with great delight that I recently trundled off with my portable chiropractic table to treat the cast of *The Wizard of Oz*. "Wizard" Mickey Rooney and "Wicked Witch" Eartha Kitt, two show business legends, had been electrifying Toronto audiences during a three-week run of this classic tale.

I never know in advance who wants care; the cast members simply write their names down on a sign-up sheet outside the stage door. Lithe "Catwoman" Eartha Kitt was a regular patient, but Mickey Rooney never requested my services. Maybe the Wizard had his own magic potion for staying flexible and pain-free.

While treating various cast members, I had discreetly managed to secure all of the key autographs for my office wall of fame, except one—the elusive Mr. Rooney. But, as with an American Express card, I had no intentions of leaving without it! Over a three-week period I had gleaned the following information: Mickey can be unpredictable, temperamental, difficult, and moody; he keeps to himself, disappears into his hotel suite right after the

I feel joyful when I tell my wife how much I love her each day.
                                        Marv, research and development

show, and definitely doesn't like to be hounded for autographs. In other words, this Emmy and Academy Award recipient, star of over 300 films and 100 television shows, and Broadway show-stopper would be a pushover for a risk-taker like me!

One day I treated an injured scarecrow, several munchkins, a flying monkey, two witches, and Dorothy. When I had finished weaving my chiropractic wizardry, there were still 30 minutes before showtime. Should I or shouldn't I? The gutsy me shouted "Go for it," while the reticent me weighed the consequences of pestering a superstar. I grabbed my poem "Use the Good Dishes," hummed a few bars from "I'm Off to See the Wizard," and found Mickey's dressing room. Surprisingly, the door was wide open. There he was, "the legend," sitting on a chair watching a movie from the 1940s. His eyes brightened when he finally noticed me.

"I love chiropractors!" he gushed after I introduced myself. "My chiropractor works on me regularly back home, especially now after my hip surgery." His unexpected warmth and friendliness disarmed me and we chatted with ease. Feeling considerably bolder now that we seemed to be best friends, I made my move. "I am writing a book called *Use the Good Dishes* and I would love to include your personal philosophy on how you celebrate life each day." I then handed him an autographed copy of my poem. After he read it, he sighed, then looked up as though searching for some inspirational words among the ceiling tiles. We spoke right up until five minutes before the curtain rose, when it was definitely time for me to leave. With a hug and a profound thank you I left, scarcely believing what had happened. I had taken a huge risk. Mickey could have complained to the producer and I would have been banished from the theatre like a wicked witch. Instead, he welcomed me. This was either a tiny miracle from the Land of Oz, or just a combination of chutzpah, good timing, and serendipity.

Here is Mickey Rooney's recipe for using the good dishes:

"Life is like a cafeteria. In life there are so many good dishes to choose from to satisfy our hunger. Good dishes come in many

I love to be surrounded by fresh flowers in my home.

Susan, salesperson

forms. There are dishes of love, friendship, sincerity, and trust. Forgiveness is one of the most beautiful dishes. There are also bad dishes like wars and murder, and dirty dishes like pornography. I'm not talking about sex. There's nothing dirty about the dish of sex.

"Human beings seem to be suffering from a chronic case of indigestion: From having too much, wanting too much, asking too much, claiming too much, inflaming too much. The solution? We must find the recipe for peace and serve it regularly. Who is ready to taste these morsels?

"Really, there is only one ultimate dish—the dish with all the answers. God is this dish. Spiritual awareness simmers in the soul of man. We will never regret having filled our soul with this.

"Start with an empty dish, because empty dishes require you to fill them with your own recipe for life, good or bad, wherever you are on your own personal journey."

HOW TO EAT AN ELEPHANT

The Utah Health and Fitness Spa hiking brochure read, "These vigorous climbs involve rough terrain, rock scrambling, bouldering, exposed areas, climbing with ropes. A high level of fitness and no fear of heights are essential. Frequent steep inclines of 1000 to 2000 feet. Approximately 11- to 13-mile adventure climbs..." It wasn't kidding.

I nearly flunked adventure climbing, deciding instead that I wanted to *live* to celebrate my next birthday. But now that this ordeal is over I'm keen to write about the experience. It seems I got stuck between more than just a rock and a hard place. Here's what happened: Two guides led our group—six muscular (check out the quads and calves!) experienced climbers plus me (fit but a first-timer) —through desert brush, lava rocks, and sandy trails to the base of the first climb. My heart was getting an aerobic

I hold hands with my wife when we walk together.

Stan, retired

workout just watching the "Fearless Six" take the lead and effort-
lessly scale the ridged red rocks of Snow Canyon to a flat ledge.
Then it was my turn. With one guide yelling instructions from
the top ledge, and one coaxing me from below, I inched my way
up, digging the toe of my boots into tiny crevices, using my hands
and knees to crawl like a crab. Midway up, I froze. The rock was
too steep. I couldn't manoeuvre my toes, legs, butt, or arms anywhere for leverage. My arms were beginning to tire. Someone up
top quickly lowered a rope to rescue me. With a tug and a pull, I
was hoisted to safety. A few minutes' rest to gulp some water,
then on to the next challenge—the chimney. Picture a vertical
passageway between two enormous mountains, a space so narrow
anyone would feel squished. For this type of climb, the only technique is to dig each foot into the sides of the crevice and use your
arms and shoulders to raise your body.

"This is impossible!" I whimpered. Bill Richey, 62, marathon
runner and hiking guide extraordinaire, soothed me. "Elaine, you
can't eat an elephant all at one sitting, either. But if you eat an elephant bite by bite, pretty soon you've eaten the whole thing. Just
focus step by step, inch by inch, and you'll make it." I summoned
up a shot of adrenalin and an ounce of optimism and dug in. With
surprising ease I reached the opening at the top. I was beginning
to feel a little cocky. And that's when I saw it. The scene facing me
was right out of an Indiana Jones adventure—the dreaded chasm!
Terrified, I looked down. Instant death! A 50-foot drop to the
bottom. A measly five-foot jump across the abyss would land me
safely on a flat shelf. Shouts of "C'mon, Elaine. You can do it!" did
not budge me. Just five feet to freedom, yet I feared that my legs
weren't capable of stretching that far. Is it only in the movies that
stunt doubles appear at moments like this to bail out the star?
Finally Bill spoke, and I wasn't in the mood to hear any more of
his motivational elephant stories.

"I have a philosophy for living to a ripe old age, " he explained.
"Know what your limits are and be safe." I knew what my limits

Each morning I get up at dawn to absorb the freshness of a new day.
Brian, engineer

were and I had just passed them. Bill climbed down to an almost invisible notch about one foot below the ledge. Then he flung his lithe body across the gap until he touched the side where I was standing. "Walk on my back!" he ordered. Trembling, I placed one foot on his strong lower back. Then I was yanked to terra firma amid cheers from the group. Bill joked, "You've just experienced the adventure climber's 4-S method of weight loss: We *scare* it off or *scrape* it off. Or we get you *stuck* in a narrow channel so you *starve* it off!"

I was now ready for something really tough, like a massage at the spa. "Which way is home?" I asked. We made our way down a winding path to a flat valley. "We're going to continue farther this way, " Bill answered, pointing to another formidable mountain to the left. "Follow this path to the right and you'll find the main road."

I walked alone, reflecting on the experience. I concluded that although I hadn't quite "gone the full distance" I did not feel like a failure. Every time we try something that we thought we could never do, we are forever changed by the effort. Our physical and emotional pursuits always teach us something about ourselves. I had definitely stretched my boundaries. Often just showing up for something that you perceive to be scary can be quite an accomplishment.

Steve Burns would agree. Always a little afraid of flying, he decided to take flying lessons after attending an exhibition that featured ultralight airplanes. "I felt I would lose some of my fear," he said. "Well, after ten lessons and being scared to death each time, I stopped doing it. I didn't win that one. Just trying something that challenges you is important. I don't have to win every time."

Fear is a natural and normal emotion that affects us physiologically and psychologically. We have all felt a racing heartbeat or queasy stomach just contemplating something that we fear. Making a speech, finding a lump, or flying in a severe thunderstorm

When I pick up my daughter from her weekend job, we have a one-hour drive together to talk about anything and everything.

Joe, teacher

are circumstances in which we might feel afraid. Fear is beneficial; we need it as a protective mechanism. For the cause of self-preservation we set our limits based on our perceptions and past experiences. As a result of a near-drowning when I was eight, I am wary when swimming in a lake or ocean, and prefer to stay close to shore. I make no apologies for this. But fear can therefore be very restrictive, and keep us trapped in a box labelled "Our Safe World." We must be willing to lift the lid and venture out. Though fears have chased me throughout my whole life—fear of the dark when I was a kid, fear of heights, fear of flying in small airplanes, fear of falling—once a fear is faced and demystified, one can apply the experience to other parts of one's life. Becoming an athlete at 29 opened my mind to new possibilities. My confidence exploded as I trained consistently and persistently for 17 marathons. New challenges beckoned to me. I was ready to test my potential—to stretch and reach. Canoeing in deep water was a personal triumph. Writing a book was another cathartic rush of victory. When my girlfriend Andrea asked me to join an indoor rock climbing group I agreed immediately. By the end of the day I was scaling a forty-five-foot wall. For the past year I have been working out with a personal trainer. Sprouting muscles makes me feel physically strong, and that strength spills over into other parts of my psyche.

Articulating and then dissecting our fears can diminish their powerful hold. Psychotherapist Shelley Stein counsels many clients who are fearful. "I try to flesh out what the real fear is; for example, 'I fear I'll lose my job' or 'I fear my wife won't love me.' I draw a big iceberg and label it fear. Then we take an imaginary pickaxe and break it down into smaller, manageable pieces. If fear is monumental, then people stay stuck."

I regularly treat patients who participate in extreme sports—those adrenalin-lovers who push the limits of their sanity while heli-skiing or scaling a sheer rock face. Have you ever wondered how your worst nightmare could be someone else's fun? Our fears come from how we perceive potentially frightening situations

Every week I buy my sweetheart her favourite chocolate truffles wrapped in gold foil.

David, business owner

rather than from the situations themselves, and our fear threshold is determined by a combination of factors, including personality, skill, and gender. Males, who are greater risk-takers than females, are more likely to consider whether the benefit of a potentially dangerous caper is worth the risk. Females tend to base their decisions on whether they may get hurt. Skill level is the most important factor in determining a fear response. Once you've mastered a sport, pushing yourself further often becomes the norm. Take, for example, Andrea Kraus, who was probably born wearing running shoes. Active her whole life in track, tennis, swimming, and gym, she easily slid into short-distance triathlon competitions in her early thirties. It wasn't too much of a reach for her to try a half-Ironman—six hours of swimming, biking, and running. Her next goal? "My half-Ironman is in my fun zone," she explained. "Now I'm exploring adventure racing—a multi-sport, multi-day, team competition involving orienteering, where you're armed with only a compass and a map." Events include kayaking or canoeing, mountain biking, hiking, bushwhacking/trekking/running, and ascending or rappelling from mountains using ropes. How did Andrea feel competing in her first race? "The rope work was scary. But if you focus on the fear, you'll panic and make a mistake. I just block it out, get past it, and work on the task at hand." Sports excellence has positively influenced how she copes with life and work issues. "Business challenges become easier to handle, plus little hassles don't bother you when you look at the big picture of life."

Gordon McClellan shares Andrea's passion for sports. He began skiing at age six and raced competitively as a schoolboy and university student. An avid fan of ski films featuring off-the-beaten-path stuff, this busy lawyer in his forties pursued skiing on terrain where exposed, 50-degree descents on faces, chutes, and couloirs of 2500 to 3500 vertical feet are common. "While heli-skiing in Alaska, no matter how cold the day, my palms and the soles of my feet were frequently moist with fear. I loved it. How seldom in life do we operate at the point where intellect

To keep my past travels to Latin America fresh in my heart, I listen to Latin music and sing along.

D'Arcy, labour educator

and instinct meet. I feel empowered when I conquer a challenge."
Like Andrea, Gordon's life skills have been strengthened through
sport. "When life confronts me with something daunting, I imagine myself looking down the walls of a couloir with an incline of
50 degrees for 3000 vertical feet. I say to myself, 'You've been
here; you've faced way scarier stuff than this. What is there to be
afraid of?'" Gordon strongly feels he's become a better person
through skiing: "Mentally tough," he says. "Most of all, facing
fear has given me an expanded sense of what is truly possible."

Greg Davisson, the Utah hiking guide who accompanied me
on my adventure climb, is normally assigned to the most super-fit
group of hikers. When I asked him to describe his most memorable
group hike, his answer surprised me. "Actually, I learned a valuable life lesson when my hiking director asked me to take a group
of unfit, overweight guests on a *walk*. I grumbled to myself, imag-
ining that this was going to be a slow, trying effort." Twelve people
showed up, with health problems ranging from obesity to vascular
disease. They set out for the West Canyon Overlook—a two-mile
walk involving mostly flat roads and some sandy trails culminat-
ing in one moderate incline with a breathtaking view. Greg stayed
with the slowest walker, a 60-year-old woman with diabetes who
weighed about 300 pounds. "She had heard how pretty the
Overlook was and was determined to see it. She asked me to help
her get to the top, to be her crutch. She stood behind me and
placed her hands on my shoulders for support. I would take a step
and stop and she would take a step and stop to catch her breath.
It seemed to take forever as we inched our way up that slope. As
we neared the top, with the rest of the group cheering her on,
she began to cry with *joy*. I had a lump in my throat listening to
her sobbing behind me. She had conquered *her* Mount Everest. I
was thrilled to make a difference for her. We all have personal
Mount Everests. The important thing is to face the fear, take that
first step, and keep going. It's in the doing that you learn the
most!"

I crawl into my bed warmed by an electric blanket.
                              Nancy, real estate agent

METAMORPHOSIS

Judge Hugh Locke opens his mail every morning with a knife that once belonged to an 18-year-old he defended on a murder charge in 1965. The jury acquitted the youth on grounds of self-defence. "His life changed after that decision. He is now a manager at an insurance company and is married with three children. He hasn't been in trouble since." I asked Judge Locke why he kept the knife. "That young man could have chosen to follow a life of crime. This knife is a continual reminder to me that there is potential in every human being to change. If people put their mind to it, they can make changes in their life."

We need to regularly revisit the changes we've made thus far, and acknowledge what we've learned—perhaps a lesson about fear, risk, sadness, courage, and joy—and keep moving. Sometimes we get so accustomed to a change that we forget how we got there. Try to remember a major change you've made in the last ten years and commend yourself on how far you've come and the growth that resulted. What convoluted steps did you take to achieve that goal? When I asked patients to name visual reminders of positive changes in their life, their answers were insightful: a trophy for the most improved student, a diploma for completing a university degree as a mature student, before and after photographs on the fridge for achieving a weight goal, a wedding band worn by someone who could trust again, two stable teens raised and nurtured by a single mom, a treat jar filled with loonies and toonies, a medal for completing a six mile road race, a framed "termination of employment" letter hanging beside a framed dollar bill from a new business owner, a prized pen to journal thoughts and feelings, a first home after struggling to meet rent payments, a peaceful painting of a lake to prompt relaxation.

For Carl Hiebert, a photograph on the wall beside his front door is his reminder of "a momentous turning point in my healing."

I frequently take photographs of family and friends and send reprints to everyone.

Jerry, investment manager

Confined to a wheelchair after a hang-gliding accident, this adventurer discovered that he could manoeuvre his body well enough to fly in an ultralight airplane. A life-changing photograph, taken by a friend, focuses on Carl's empty wheelchair parked by a field, with Carl waving from his airplane as he flies overhead. "That photograph has remained the most emotionally charged picture of my life, vibrant in its tension between the empty wheelchair and my wave of jubilation," he says. "Had my whole identity been tied up in my physical being, this accident might have been devastating. My challenge was to keep my mind and spirit alive, for they knew nothing of the limitations of wheelchairs." Carl has been on a limitless journey ever since.

Do you have something visible that reminds you of the power of change? Find a new dream that stirs your imagination or stimulates creative energy, something that prompts you to focus in a new direction. Baby boomers by the thousands are heading for the exits as a result of downsizing and early retirement packages. What are you going to do for the next 30 or 40 years? Here is where the creative juices take over. Explore avenues that encourage you to reinvent yourself.

Rabbi Bernard Baskin, 80, shared his wisdom to help those looking at transitions in life. "Everything about us is undergoing transformation, a metamorphosis. A mature person understands they can't remain in a rut. But some people make no provision for change." Rabbi Baskin certainly did. After retiring from Temple Anshe Sholom, he and his wife started a book business. "I have a library of over 10,000 books. We now have 18 catalogues with 500 books each for our mail-order business. We're travelling all over to buy libraries from colleagues. You'll even find us on the Internet." And how should we adapt to change? "A person who wants to live most fully must come to terms with transition within ourselves and the society around us. We age, which means we change physically, we change emotionally, and as time goes on we change spiritually, reaching out in new areas to find meaning.

Every day I sing, play the piano, and listen to classical music.
                                                                    Ruth, cantor

It's important when we set goals to realize that we can't always achieve them. Life is a process and the real meaning is in the journey."

I have a framed newspaper article on the wall in front of my desk. It's from the *Toronto Star* dated June 16, 1994, one year before my book *Passionate Longevity* was published. The subject of the article was the publishing business. The vice-president of Macmillan was quoted as saying, "Of the unsolicited manuscripts of which we get about 3000 a year, we probably publish three." Well, I was one of those three! I went from chiropractor to author, never doubting that I would find a publisher. That keeps me going!

If you are looking for a suggestion to help you make a significant change right away, remove the good dishes from the china cabinet and keep them in the kitchen. Using the good dishes every day may just be the best reminder of all—that life is fragile, precious, fleeting, unpredictable, and ever-changing.

LIFE IS MOTION

When he was nine years old, Dr. Robert Salter, world-renowned orthopedic surgeon and a teacher and scientist at Toronto's Hospital for Sick Children, observed something that would later drive him to challenge the very roots of traditional medical thinking. "My twin brother was sick with rheumatic fever," he recalled. "There was only one treatment at that time: bed rest for one year. He slowly deteriorated before my eyes, becoming weaker and weaker. I could see that immobilizing someone was bad." It was then that young Robert decided to become a doctor in the hope of one day discovering something better. A decade later at university, he again experienced the same lesson, only this time he was the patient. "Orthopedic surgeons always wanted to put me into a cast for my frequent sports injuries. When I

I work shifts, so I look forward to dinner together as a family four times a week.

Dee, customer service representative

stayed away from them, my joint injuries healed faster and with better motion."

In 1955, with great determination, courage, and a willingness to venture beyond traditional wisdom, he began doing research on the harmful effects of immobilizing joints, which was then a universally accepted medical therapy. "In 1970, in keeping with Aristotle's philosophy that motion is life and life is motion, I went even further into the unknown by conceiving a revolutionary idea: The best treatment for disease and injured joints would be *continuous passive motion* (CPM). This would require a machine to provide motion for at least a few weeks to facilitate the healing process." Not surprisingly, he faced considerable skepticism and opposition from fellow scientists and surgeons. "Nothing in the body moves all the time," they challenged. "What about the heart?" Dr. Salter refuted. "Well, there are no joints in the body that move all the time," they retorted. "Yes, the joints between our ribs and spine move with each breath, lasting a whole lifetime," Dr. Salter argued. Steadfast, he proved through almost 30 years of research that his theory is correct. To date, CPM has benefited 5 million patients in 15,000 hospitals in 57 countries worldwide.

Dr. Salter has always been adventurous, and eager to discover new things. "I wasn't afraid to risk my reputation as a scientist because I believed that my thinking was right." Quoting Schopenhauer, he said, "Every new idea goes through three phases: Ridicule, resistance, and considered self-evident!" Then, with a laugh, Dr. Salter asked me if I knew the Roman rule: "The one who says it's impossible should never interrupt the one who's doing it!" Dr. Salter has a passionate plea for graduating medical students: "Imagine something new. Question dogma. Explore where there is no path and leave a trail that leads into the future."

Dr. Salter's discovery can serve as a metaphor for our lives. Immobility is not only harmful for our body but for our spirits as well. We were designed to move emotionally, physically, and

I sing in the shower every morning.

Harry, scientist

spiritually. Some individuals wear invisible body casts that restrain them. They choose to stay in an unhappy relationship or career rather than venture into the unknown. Or they spend years complaining about how miserable they are, unable to act, or waiting for circumstances to force them to move. Why? "Fear of loss," according to Roger Gabriel, director of education for the Chopra Center for Wellbeing in La Jolla, California. "We can't be happy if there is a lot of fear in our life. And the fear is always of loss. We get so attached and addicted to the roles that we play—businesswoman, husband—if we think these roles are all there is then we get into trouble when they're gone. As a result, we hang on to things, people, and circumstances for control, approval, and power—all out of fear. When our happiness is not tied to external objects and we are happy within ourselves, then we can move towards any challenge."

Avoiding risk is like going through life not plugged in. Your screen is blank. There is no history to be savoured or saved. However, many of us are moving forward, breaking new ground, paving our own trails to create our future. Life journeys are seldom linear; our footsteps often take us on a meandering path. And that's where we learn the most about ourselves. Leave the safety of a well-worn route. Acknowledge your sweaty palms. Accept that you may feel ambivalent as a new opportunity, challenge, or change presents itself. Are there any "boogeymen" blocking your trail? Go around them. Or move sideways for as long as you need to, then climb higher, or dig deeper. Just move. Staying still is just as bad as going backwards.

Carl Hiebert's life reflects a journey of risk. He pursued adventure sports, from scuba diving to sky diving, until a freak hang-gliding accident in 1981 left him a paraplegic. Undaunted, he realized that he had been presented with the challenge of his life, and that it was his responsibility to make the best of it. After several months in the hospital, followed by only two weeks of rehabilitation, he hung a "Gone Flying" sign on his hospital door. With

I bake with chocolate—cookies, cakes, and tarts.
                                    Mervin, *retired accountant*

the help of his hang-gliding buddy, Carl left his wheelchair behind, taking off in a single-seat ultralight airplane. "As I buzzed the field and saw my empty wheelchair below, I was overcome. Even if I couldn't walk, I could still fly!" In 1986, Carl became the first Canadian to fly across Canada in an ultralight plane. His book *The Gift of Wings* features his journal and the stunning aerial landscapes that he photographed during that trip. Meeting Carl was an unforgettable experience. I was inspired by his courage, tenacity, and wit. What is his philosophy of risk? "Risk-taking is simply the willingness to explore the unknown, even when we don't have all of the answers. What perhaps separates risk-takers from those who hold back is the decision to focus on the goal and not on the fear. We can run from fear or choose to meet it head on. It's a matter of personal choice, and each of us is ultimately responsible for our own decision. We are all capable of doing more and being greater than we are. But these discoveries will never happen unless we put ourselves to the test."

Bernie Klein has never been afraid to test himself. At an age when many people think about retiring, this 62-year-old entrepreneur recently started a new company that went public. "I've had failures in my life, both in business and in relationships," he said. "Failure is not a bad thing, but not trying is. Nearly everything in our lives—love, business—involves risk. In order to win in life, we need courage, determination, and a sense of adventure to explore what is out there for all of us. And failure is part of that learning process."

"Arctic" Joe Womersley, 74, war veteran, marathon runner, Ironman triathlete, entrepreneur, and lover of life (and women), has always "explored where there is no path leaving a trail that leads into the future." When I asked Joe about taking risks in life, he summed it all up in three words. Put them on a Post-it note and stick it to your bathroom mirror so you can read them each morning: GO FOR BROKE!!

I rise at dawn to see the early morning light.

Judy, teacher

GROWING PAINS

I look back on my childhood with ambivalence. Back then, life ranged from ecstatic to traumatic depending on what was happening with my parents. My father was 54 when I was born, a grey-haired genius of sorts, an inventor and entrepreneur. He wheeled and dealed in war surplus, speculated on land and stocks, and gambled on horses. Creativity was encouraged; new ideas bounced off the walls in our animated household. His two mottoes were: "All you need is one good idea" and "Be your own boss." He was a risk-taker to the very heart of his adventurous spirit. Change was the norm for my family: We moved eight times before I left home for university. Mom was more of a stabilizing force. Although she was not in good health, she was always at home, cooking, taking care of Steven and me, and worrying about my dad's schemes.

I understand now how these early experiences carve out a model for our lives—for how we think, act, and feel. As adults, we either duplicate our family histories or rebel against them, forgetting even their good parts.

There is a third choice, says marital and family therapist Reesa Kassirer. "If we complete our journey of understanding and accepting our parents, not as mother and father, but as human beings with vulnerabilities, then we are free to choose the best parts of our history and live it." With maturity, we can then stand back and select what fits for us.

Candice Rice was raised by an unadventurous mom and a dad who loved to travel, and she decided early how she wanted to live. "My mom never learned to drive and was totally dependent on Dad. I heard her fret, 'I don't think I can do it' or 'It's too late to learn.' She didn't want to go anywhere, complaining, 'It's too far, too expensive, and I don't want to eat the food.' As a result, my dad postponed his travel plans." In contrast to the way her mother lived, Candice got her driver's licence at 18, then left

I sit in the backyard watching my family play.

Ebie, mother

home at 20, moving from Montreal to Vancouver. "Mom wanted me to be a nurse, just like her. I didn't want to do that." So after university, Candice became a trade consultant for the government, which required frequent travel. After her mother died, Candice's father (at 69) was finally able to rekindle his passion for travel. "He announced that he was going to Florida, but unfortunately he seriously hurt his back in a car accident and was unable to go anywhere. The last 11 years of his life were very restricted." After he died, Candice found among his personal effects several travel articles describing the scenic California coast. "He often talked about driving from Los Angeles to San Francisco. He never made it, but I've resolved to do what I want to do now and not put it off." Before Candice and her family left for the California coast, she booked a Christmas cruise and a summer holiday in England.

Penny Thomsen learned from her family to love change at an early age. "My father was in the Canadian Armed Forces, so while I was growing up we lived in seven different cities across the country. My optimistic parents taught me to view change as an exciting opportunity, not to fear it or dread it. I easily made new friends and learned to feel comfortable in strange situations. If you wait for the perfect time to have a baby, change jobs, or start a new career, you'll never do it. I'd rather move today with a good plan than wait forever for a perfect plan. You'll fine-tune it as it goes. We can never know all of the variables, so be comfortable with ambiguity, especially in today's evolving world." How much does this distance runner love change? "I'd move my furniture every day if I could!"

Our teachers can also be powerful mentors, influencing the way that we think and feel from an early age. Steve Burns credits his grade ten algebra teacher with "having an impact on the way I work today; the way I tick." His teacher would regularly assign a half-dozen math questions from the easy A section, about two or three questions from the B section, and only one question from the

I treat myself to chocolate-covered gingers.

Helen, writer

very difficult C section. Steve recalled his teacher's special method to challenge and motivate students. "He offered to buy a milkshake in the cafeteria for anybody who got the answer to the C question. Well, those were the only ones I tackled. I'd keep at it even if it meant staying up 'til four in the morning. He threw down the gauntlet and I was there. True to his word, he'd buy me a milkshake the next day. Even today, I'm not happy unless I'm challenged. I can't do the pedestrian stuff."

Neither can I. At 20, I quit university and took a huge leap into the unknown. I started a crocheted jewellery fashion fad that I knew would have a limited shelf life, but did it anyway, loving the challenge and excitement of running my own business. It was over at 23. Undaunted, I went back to school at 25, to become a chiropractor. My dad taught me well—I had to be my own boss. What have I learned from this? With every dream, change, and challenge comes a "growth spurt" accompanied by pains. That's how life is. When we spread our wings, we inevitably stretch our emotional tendons. They ache for a while until we get used to their new dimensions. And then we grow some more. What happens next? According to Deborah Szekely, a 77-year-old entre-preneur who in 1940 conceived of a health spa that has since mushroomed into Mexico's successful Rancho La Puerta, "As long as you are growing, learning, being productive, finding and surmounting challenges, you are definitely not growing old. You are, in fact, growing *up*." Incidentally, she is so certain that one's "second half" of life is a time of dreams, growth, change, and choices that she is now starting a magazine for those people who have made major lifestyle changes "past 40, or 50, or 80!" Their examples, Deborah feels, will help others to find the courage to change.

Every summer I have a garden party, for about 30 special women in various stages of growing *up*. This celebration of friendship began 12 years ago, initially as a tribute to the girlfriends who comforted me after my separation. Now this annual ritual has

For the last 20 years I've kept a daily diary filled with thoughts and events of the day.

Mary, retired

evolved into a sharing of all of our life journeys. Each year I dream up a question that requires my friends to ponder lessons learned in the previous year. Each woman, ranging in age from 25 to 70, stands up and tells her story. I have found them eager to disclose their issues, and grateful to learn how others have somehow changed their lives. For the younger women in the group, life stories are often mixed with angst, hopes of "getting there," upheavals in relationships, and uncertainty about the future. At this year's party, the voices from my age group were strong and confident. Many of the women in their fifties celebrated break-throughs in career and relationships. Most striking was the over-whelming sense of acceptance of oneself—a caring about how they feel, rather than about what others think. "I am connected to who I am and what I am," revealed one friend, capturing the feelings of many of us.

And what is the essence of being 50? For me it has meant exploring my inner life, cultivating my creative endeavours, and finding meaning spiritually. I often struggle with learning to value the process, detaching myself from outcomes, and living in the present, but at least I'm conscious of how crucial these are for my equanimity. Most of all, I feel contentment and gratitude for my life, yet I am always eager and open to explore new opportuni-ties that inevitably cross my path. Hope Sealy had an epiphany at 50 and just stopped being fearful. "I wasn't conscious of being afraid of life. But something happened in my fifties, when I real-ized three things: I don't have to be afraid, I am what I am, and what I am is evolving, so to hell with everything else!"

Many people share my sentiments. They express their need for solitude, their belief in the importance of friendships, and their realization of their own mortality. At this time in our lives we finally choose to "do it now," whether the "it" means beginning a new career, simplifying one's living space, pursuing creative interests, or changing one's marital status. Even for those who feel they have to consider others first—children, parents, spouse—

I appreciate my loving husband, who makes me breakfast in bed every morning.

June, writer-broadcaster

50 and older can still signal a tremendous sense of freedom as they pursue what is in their hearts.

DUSTING OFF THE GOOD DISHES

You are constantly evolving and changing, even though you might not be aware of it. After re-examining her life, a 55-year-old patient said, "I'd never want to be 30 again!" Who you were at 30, your issues, values, passions, and the relationships you attracted into your life may be vastly different from who you are now. We must remember that that was our reality then. Now wiser, many of us looking back from the other side of 50 cringe or laugh at the sometimes crazy choices and beliefs that defined us when we were younger. Where are you now? Given unlimited money and time, would you continue to pursue your current work? Are you on a path that feels natural for you?

Ruth Stern asked herself these questions after 25-plus years in the fashion industry. When her last position ended, her exit agreement included career counselling. Although for ten years Ruth had felt that her values no longer matched her chosen field, it was Paul Giroux, a transition coach, who helped her explore a new direction. "Initially I was scared, " she admitted, "because I was walking away from my identity. My heart and gut told me it was time to move on. I wasn't sure how to utilize my 'merchant instinct' skills and apply them differently, but Paul opened me up to new possibilities. I knew I wanted to help people and sensed a whole renaissance in the wellness field." Ruth is now happily ensconced in the health and wellness industry.

I asked Paul Giroux how he helps people to reinvent themselves. "My clients are in various stages of transition and may be confused, fearful, or lost. Something has been taken away from them, a job or a title, and they come searching for answers to external questions. They leave with questions about themselves,

Before I go to bed each night, I go to my three boys' bedrooms and kiss them on the forehead.

Steve, accountant

about who they are and what really matters in their life. I help
them 'dust off the good dishes' by rewriting and rebuilding their
life stories." We can imagine for a moment that *we* are the good
dishes. Dust will settle with inertia and dull one's true essence. The
brilliance and sparkle is always there, but sometimes you just need
a polishing. "It is time to tell your story in a new way," Paul
believes.

For those really lost individuals, Paul says, "I have to first help
them find the cartons with the good dishes, unpack them, and
then dust them off!" Paul believes as I do that people have inside
themselves everything they need to solve their problems and be
truly happy. "We have to first nurture and love ourselves and
then we can love others." he believes. "I appreciate the people who
unexpectedly come into my life, and the surprises that come my
way. We can even learn from the interruptions. I'm open—that's
how I live my life." Indeed, a chance meeting can alter your perception, or a sentence in a book can open you up to new insights.
Listening to advice from friends or family that we previously
ignored (getting fit, practising meditation) can also change your
life.

How do we dust off the good dishes when life hands us
challenges?

1. Take time to consider what has happened. We can fight
   obstacles, which usually creates more chaos, or we can
   encourage our minds to slowly shift from "why?" to "why
   not?" and learn from the experience. We need time to
   regroup, absorb, and digest what the universe has handed us.
   Roger Gabriel, director of education at the Chopra Center
   for Wellbeing, explains this process by describing the actions
   of a bow and arrow: "If you want an arrow to shoot forward
   with dynamism, you need to pull the arrow *back* and take it
   in the other direction. Then let it go and it travels. If you
   put an arrow on a bow and let it go, it just falls to the

*For breakfast each morning I eat homemade bread toasted crisp with
fresh marmalade on top.*

                                                    Doris, *artist*

ground. We can't always be charging forward. Withdraw, assimilate, and the clarity will come."

2. Raise the bar. In order to grow we must push ourselves out of our comfort zone and stretch further than we imagined possible. Know your limits, as well, or disappointment and failure will accompany you.

3. Do what is in your heart without needing approval from others. Sharon Allen, a gallery director in La Jolla, California, decided to leave her safe boundaries and venture into the unknown. "I was in an 'okay' marriage for 15 years. Then I met John, who was like an electric charge jolting me out of my mediocre relationship. Too often we stay where we are to please others, to make them or ourselves feel safer. When you do something totally unpredictable, it shakes everything up. Be gutsy and do it. My life has been an amazing adventure!"

4. Be patient. This is the toughest challenge of all. You can't stand over a plant and make it grow faster. There is a natural rhythm to every living thing. Goals are necessary but rigidity hampers growth. As Roger Gabriel says, "When we are fixed and obsessed with an end result or desire, we close ourselves to other possibilities. Maybe there is another opportunity you are not even aware of yet. Trust the universe and get out of the way."

I meet my running buddies each morning for a group run.

Bill, judge

GIVING

Gifts

Said Grandma to her family, "Here's what we really need.
Our home is overcrowded, no more stuff, I plead.
We'd love some homemade cookies, or dinner at your place,
Contribute to our charity, or wood for our fireplace.
To our beloved grandchildren, I'll teach you how to sew.
We'll read a book together, or watch a video.
We wouldn't mind some tickets to a concert or a play,
A few stamps for letters, or tokens for the subway.
Grandpa's socks are thinning, you know I hate to darn.
The dishtowels need replacing. I'd love some wool or yarn
To knit a scarf or sweater that reminds me of the snow
Lend a hand with the shovelling, we'd appreciate it so.
Help us plant bulbs, pull weeds, and cut the grass.
Kids, there's milk and cookies, when you visit after class.
A long-distance phone card, some film or birdseed,
School photos for our wallets bring a smile, indeed.
A Sunday walk together, a bouquet of fresh flowers.
You can't buy what we'd love most, a present of hours,
Just to spend time, to chat and have some tea,
Using our good dishes, for us it's heavenly.
The things that really matter can't fit in drawers or shelves,
Though we're grateful for small gifts, the best ones
are yourselves!"

As I write this, there are only 12 days until Christmas. Stores are packed with frantic shoppers wondering what to buy for their loved ones. The older I get, the more I realize that what many of us really want isn't for sale. As a patient of mine said after I read her my poem, "All I want is a gift of time. My daughter works

I sit on my front porch in the morning, sipping tea and contemplating my day.

Phyllis, artist

two jobs, has a husband and house to look after. I'd give anything to have a coffee with her alone, just to chat for an hour!"

My memories of this past Hanukkah have little to do with what I received. Instead, I'll remember my brother Steven and his wife, Cheryl, using their computer to create a delightful little illustrated storybook for their beautiful 20-month-old granddaughter, Tovah. I cried while reading that simple story about a small tulip that grew tall with nourishment from the sun and rain. I also loved receiving photos of Joel, 15, and Adam, 13, who are becoming young men before my eyes. Though the gifts I received were all appreciated, what was most meaningful was my family's reaction to what I gave them. I was most touched to see Tovah in the outfit I had bought for her: pink fleece bell-bottom pants with an embroidered red heart on the top, and a matching barrette. The giving was more special than the getting.

Mary Bourn understands my sentiments. On her ninetieth birthday, this dear friend gave *me* a present—a delicious-smelling still-warm fruit bread that she had just baked that morning! As soon as I walked into her apartment, I could smell the unmistakable aroma of something in the oven.

"For me?" I asked, with a mixture of awe and disbelief.

"It's an 82-year-old custom that my parents initiated, called a reverse birthday," Mary explained. "When I was eight, two bratty kids next door would announce way in advance what they wanted on their birthday. My parents said, 'That's not going to happen at our house' and then came up with the reverse birthday, where on your birthday, you give something to someone you like. When I was young, I would make a gift like a poem or a picture. I learned from an early age the importance of giving to others." Mary gives so much to family and friends with her sunny personality and ready laugh that we all wanted to give her something. Her apartment was filled with gorgeous flowers from everyone on the occasion of her landmark birthday. Call it a *reversed* reverse birthday!

I dance in my living room to oldies music.

Dorothy, teacher

Magda Klein's four sons wanted to do something special for her to mark her eighty-fifth birthday in February. So they plotted a surprise one-day visit to Florida, where she spends the winter. They told her that only Danny would be visiting for a couple of days, and that the other three sons couldn't be there for the occasion. Danny needed to sneak out to the airport to pick up his brothers without Magda finding out where he was going, so on the morning of her birthday, Danny returned from a walk with a perfect excuse. He announced that he had met a woman on the boardwalk and was going to have coffee with her. This did not please Magda.

"Danny," she pleaded, "you're only here two days. Don't go now. I haven't seen you and I want to talk to you."

Danny insisted that he had to go and left the apartment. About an hour later, the four sons silently tiptoed down the apartment corridor, but only Danny entered the apartment.

"Mom," he said with a smile, "I want you to meet the woman I met this morning." Bernie, Reuben, and Eli walked in without a word. Magda was sitting in the dining room with her back to the door. She turned with a stern look, expecting to see the woman who was intruding on this brief visit with her son. Instead, she cried with joy on seeing her three sons. Now, over a year later, Magda still talks about this surprise as the best gift she has ever received.

Think about someone you care about. What do they really want from you that cannot be bought? What would make them happy? Here are some suggestions:

- Write a heartfelt poem or a letter expressing your love.
- Make them a special dinner (and clean up afterwards).
- Go out for coffee regularly and just chat.
- Create some coupons with chores on them; for example, "I will clean out the basement storage room, give you a massage once a week, and listen for five minutes without speaking."

I use my fanciest tea cups and silver every day.

Jane, consultant

If you do want to spend some money, here are a few more suggestions:

- Treat them to a manicure or pedicure.
- Take their car in to be winterized.
- Plant dozens of tulip bulbs in their yard.
- Have some photos taken and get them framed.

It doesn't take much to give many of us joy in everyday life.

The most meaningful gifts come from the heart. Giving is about the small joys that we receive in our life and the people who give them to us. There are gifts of compassion—volunteering to help others in need—and gifts of friendship. Touch says so much—a gift of a comforting hand on someone's shoulder, or holding hands with someone you love. Giving explores the gift of just being a decent human being—polite, respectful, caring. Finally, what gifts do you want to give to the future generation? What values, traditions, and memories do you want to give those who come after us? Giving benefits to us all, J.M. Barrie wrote in a poem: "Those who bring sunshine to the lives of others cannot keep it from themselves."

HUMANNESS

"Use the Good Dishes" is about celebrating the small, ordinary things that often go unnoticed. More importantly, it is also about appreciating the people who bring us those small joys. When you value and cherish the people who give to you, then you will gladly bring joy into other people's lives with the same generosity of spirit. If you love fresh flowers, you'll be thrilled to receive them, and then, knowing how this small gesture affects you, you'll readily reciprocate.

Why is it so difficult to connect with others in a truly human way? Humanness at the most basic level involves caring about

I go to bed knowing that my kitchen counters are spotless and that the dishes in the dishwasher are clean and ready for tomorrow.

Helen, mother

others. Whether it is helping someone who appears lost, picking up a discarded pop can on the sidewalk, or just saying thanks to the kid who pumps your gas, humanness requires that you think of others. The Golden Rule—do unto others as you would have them do unto you—is the most thoughtful rule to live by. How would you react if, through some error or miscommunication, a certain seat or hotel room or service you specifically requested was unavailable? Would you yell or get nasty with the clerk who had nothing to do with the mistake? Put yourself in their shoes. Take a moment to quell any anger. Then you might want to calmly speak to the manager. If you behave in a civil yet firm way, things usually work out. For example, when I discovered that my low-fat airline meal had not been ordered, the helpful flight attendant brought me two different dinner choices so I could mix and match to satisfy my diet needs. I thanked her for her help and ingenuity.

Acknowledging the presence of others is also a human thing to do. Saying "hello" or "good morning" is so simple, and yet we've all been in an elevator with someone in total silence, staring at the floor numbers. It is beyond me how one can sit on an airplane, practically joined shoulder to shoulder with someone, and not at least acknowledge them. Even if you're tired, cranky, or need solitude, you can still smile or say hello and then put your nose in reading material or close your eyes.

There is a three-mile trail in midtown Toronto hidden behind a residential area that is known intimately to runners, walkers, and dogs. Tall bushy trees on either side of this well-worn path join to form an archway that somehow catches the sun and dazzles the eyes. On most mornings, you will hear the friendly voice of "Arctic" Joe Womersley, 74, utter his favourite two-letter word— "Hi!"—as he runs past you. "I say, 'Hi, good morning' and smile to everyone I meet during my ten-kilometre run," says this Ironman and marathon runner extraordinaire. "The highest response rate I've ever received in one run is about 82 percent. Some people who pass me on the trail look miserable and preoccupied, and never

I make my wife her favourite breakfast on the weekends—raisin, cinnamon, and nutmeg oatmeal.

Bill, *judge*

make eye contact." Joe often stops to pat a dog on the head or chat with moms pushing strollers. "I think it's my background that helped me appreciate people. Everything I have in life I had to earn. There were no freebies. I learned to be nice to people."

It is always the little things in life that mean so much, like showing appreciation for good service, or remembering someone's name. When staying in a hotel, most of us tip the porter, but how many remember to leave something for the hard-working cleaning staff? Express your gratitude by leaving an appropriate tip. Recently I ordered room service in a hotel. The waiter (who arrived five minutes early) was friendly, courteous, and funny. That brief encounter was a treat for me, so after my meal I filled out the "How did we do today?" card that the hotel had attached to the tray, mentioning the waiter's name and hoping he'd receive recognition. The next time you make a telephone call to a business, listen carefully for the name of the person who answers the phone. For example, in my office, you'll hear: "Dr. Dembe's office, Dina speaking." I make a point of repeating someone's name when I'm on the telephone. Call it the human touch.

Last year, I spoke at an early morning conference. While I was being introduced, I suddenly had an idea for my opening remarks. I asked everyone in that huge hotel ballroom to think about all of the human connections that were in synergy to make this morning event happen. "Let's acknowledge the hotel staff, who are often invisible to us," I suggested. "Dozens of men and women set the tables for breakfast, getting up in the dark to be here on time. Think of all the arrangements that had to be made for transportation, perhaps babysitters. The chef and his team had to carefully prepare 300 hot meals." Then I asked the audience to consider the special arrangements they made with family or friends to be there. There was a murmur around the room as we marvelled at the number of people who gave their time and energy to help others that morning. The next time you attend a function—perhaps a wedding, bar mitzvah, or charity fundraiser—look around

I make a point of noticing something nice about my clients so I can pay them a compliment.

Elena, hairdresser

the room. Be grateful for the hundreds of hands that were hard at work before you showed up. Don't forget to notice the gorgeous flowers arranged in the centre of each table. Smell them, too!

One of my patients described moving into a home left absolutely spotless by the previous owners. Not only were the floors washed and the carpets vacuumed, but a bouquet of spring flowers with a "Good luck in your new home" card greeted them in the sparkling kitchen. This simple act speaks volumes about respecting and caring about others.

An acquaintance, Linda Markowsky, described a peculiar yet meaningful relationship that she has enjoyed with a complete stranger. "At the corner of Church and Gerrard streets, there is a hostel for mentally ill and abused women," she explained. "For over a year, I have walked past this shelter with my dog, developing a 'looking relationship' with an old woman who sits on the porch every day. Pale, thin, and stern-looking, she stares vacantly ahead smoking her cigarettes. When I look at her from the sidewalk and smile, she breaks her gaze and always smiles back at me. We have never spoken a word, yet I have a sense that we both have stories to share with each other. I find strength and truth in this silent human connection."

Sometimes a natural disaster or an act of God will bring strangers together in a shared bond of humanity. In 1998 Montreal was struck by a devastating ice storm that littered the streets with fallen trees and left the remaining icy tree branches so weighted down, they were in danger of crashing without warning. The massive power failure forced people to revert to the good old days, before computers and television. Families cooked in their fireplace, huddled together for warmth, and talked with each other. In neighbourhoods where power was out on one side of the street but not the other, neighbours invited the have-nots over for meals and sleepovers. In contrast to the chilly air, people generated warmth by giving, reaching out, and banding together to help and care for those in need. One older woman who lived alone

I nurture and water my plants every week.

Barbara, chiropractor

borrowed a huge stockpot and invited her neighbours over for delicious homemade soup. It was the first time she had chatted with many of them. I find it telling that we can maintain an e-mail relationship with someone who lives in New Zealand, and yet haven't introduced ourselves to the people across the street. Why does it sometimes take a crisis to open our hearts and be human?

TWO HOURS, TWO COFFEES, AND SOME SHOELACES

Maybe once in a lifetime, if you are fortunate, you meet a wise, compassionate human being who touches your heart. Someone you'd like to adopt into your family so you could chat regularly about life. I hereby announce that I would like to adopt Dr. Robert Salter. He graciously granted me two separate interviews for this book; two hours out of his well-lived and well-loved 74 years. It was heartwarming to learn about his remarkable life.

As I mentioned earlier, Dr. Salter's twin brother, Jack, became ill with rheumatic fever when he was nine. Young Robert was very close to his brother, and was so distressed when he heard that Jack would need a year to recover that he spoke to the family doctor. "If Jack misses a whole year of school, he'll fall behind. I'd like to teach him the lessons he's missing every day when I come home from school." Unfortunately, the doctor felt that Jack was too sick to manage this. To make matters worse, Jack eventually lost strength in his limbs. "At the end of the year, I had to lift him out of bed each day, just to get him standing."

Determined to help his brother, Robert went to his teacher with an idea. "If I teach Jack this summer, would you at least give him a chance to make up his school year?" The teacher agreed. Overjoyed, Robert told Jack the rules at "Salter's summer school": "Every day except Sunday, from 8:00 until 2:00, I will teach you from my notes and books. After 2:00, we can go fishing or play

The look, touch, and smell of my baby's hair nurtures my soul.
Karen, mother

baseball." At the end of the summer, Jack took four exams, all of which he passed, and that September Robert and Jack entered the next grade together. "That taught me the importance of thinking of the needs of others," Dr. Salter said.

When he was 12, Dr. Salter and his family moved from their hometown of Stratford to Toronto. During the summers Robert worked hard to save money for medical school, taking jobs as a hired farmhand, digging ditches, driving rivets in a shipyard, working construction, and driving trucks. Those experiences as a labourer taught him the value of hard work. "In the hospital I appreciate everyone: the cleaners, the people who push the supply trolleys, the painters. They know me and call me by name. I care about them."

Each year, the Hospital for Sick Children recognizes and honours an individual who has demonstrated compassion and humanitarianism in providing care to children and their families. In 1999, the Staff Humanitarian Award not only was presented to Dr. Salter, but was renamed the Robert Salter Humanitarian Award, a fitting tribute to this man who has given so much to others.

Dr. Salter told me a touching story about a patient he treated 37 years ago who honoured him at the ceremony. "I operated on a baby who was born with a condition that paralyzed her lower limbs. With a series of operations over a period of years, her legs were straightened. With braces she was able to stand up and walk. Even though she was short—her legs did not have the normal growth potential—her attitude was wonderful, and she felt grateful for all of the help she was given. After graduating from university, she became a terrific social worker. Now she works at this hospital—her way of saying thank you for all of the special care she received. At the award ceremony she recalled that once, when she was ten or eleven and getting ready to leave my clinic after an examination, I noticed that her shoelaces were undone. I knew how difficult it was for her to bend her knees, so I knelt down

I love the feeling of warm water on my back in the shower.
                                          Dave, insurance broker

and tied them. She and her family remembered that incident, which I had long since forgotten."

The Shriners have a motto: "A man never stands so tall as when he stoops to help a child." Dr. Robert Salter, who has been helping children for almost his entire life, stands very tall in the hearts of everyone who knows him.

LOST FOREVER: ONE BEST FRIEND

One sunny Sunday morning, Gerry Lokash and Bobby Beder shared with me their thoughts on their almost 50-year friendship with Paul Schrieder, fraternity brother, trusted confidant, and "playmate" for life. Paul had died of cancer two weeks earlier.

"My childhood ended on July 16, 1999, the day that Paul told me he had cancer. We played in the sandbox for decades, sharing our toys," said Gerry, still raw from the death of his close friend.

"Now that Paul's gone, there's a big hole in my life that will never be filled," said Bobby, sitting across from Gerry. "I don't think we ever grew up. The great thing about our relationship was that it didn't really change as we got older."

The friendship began when the three were 11-year-old kids in public school. "Paul was big for his age and very mature," said Bobby. "He was 11 going on 18, very interested in girls. I was 11 going on 9 or 10."

Gerry added, "Paul was very confident and he sort of intimidated me at the time. Well, we all ended up in the same high school class and became good friends." University life cemented their relationship; the three bright, socially active adolescents all joined the same fraternity at the University of Toronto. "Bobby and I were more serious types," said Gerry. "Paul was more laid back, frivolous and lighter in his approach to life, which allowed us to loosen up." In the early 1960s, Paul got his pilot's licence, and the three of them would take off on jaunts for fun and adventure.

I relish seeing the sun stream through the blinds on the front window.
Edith, retired

Paul eventually became a lawyer, and Bobby and Gerry, chartered accountants. Bobby found his niche in the investment business. Gerry pursued a career in the corporate world. "Prior to setting up his law practice, Paul spent a few years as legal counsel with the investment firm I was with," said Bobby. They all followed a similar life path—getting married and having families. "Our relationship was easy to maintain since we all moved to the same neighbourhood soon after we married." Gerry said.

With busy careers and family life taking up much of their time, the three made a point of getting together regularly for Friday lunches and dinners once a month, which they termed "monthly meetings."

"My relationship with Paul," explained Gerry, "was very much like a "Seinfeld" episode. We had the most enjoyable time doing nothing. On a moment's notice—with a spontaneous phone call from any one of us—we would get together. Paul and I would go out for two- or three-hour lunches and talk about the people we knew, the economy or politics. We had all of these great ideas and we solved nothing. We used to joke that we were in the transportation business, because we loved cars, boats, and airplanes. On a nice day you might find us washing our cars, or boating or flying together. It was so easy to be together: you could relax and just be yourself. Paul and I spoke on the phone almost every day—what's doing with you?—sometimes more than once a day."

For Bobby, Paul was in some ways like a brother. "Paul was always very concerned if something was upsetting me. He would jump right in and help. Then he would make me laugh with his patented one-liners and expressions that only an insider like Gerry or me would understand."

In the spring of 1999, Paul wasn't feeling well. Lunch and dinners with his two buddies left him with what he thought was indigestion. Numerous medical tests were inconclusive. A CAT scan ultimately revealed that he had pancreatic cancer. "I remember the first moment I saw Paul just afterwards." Bobby recalled. "Paul

> Monday to Friday, for the past 20 years, my buddy John and I talk on the phone at 7 a.m. about anything and everything.
> Bernie, broker

came down the stairs in his house, opened the door, looked at me, and said, 'Dead man walking.' We were both crying. I didn't know what to do for him, except be there, be with him."

"We tried to make the most of the summer with this black cloud over our heads," said Gerry. "We would take him out for coffee or lunch as often as he wanted to go."

By the fall, Paul's condition had worsened and he spent more time in bed. "Paul always liked to talk, so we were just happy to sit there during our visits and listen to him talk," said Gerry. "It was difficult to see him changing, noticing his daily habits becoming more restrictive. Little things became so important for us—like going for a walk around the block or for a drive in the car, or just sitting in his backyard on a sunny October day. The three of us might even sit there and say nothing, but it was enough to know that we were all together, which made him feel good."

Paul Schrieder died on December 1, 1999.

"Do you have any insights on life now that you've gone through this difficult loss?" I asked.

Bobby spoke first. "Losing a childhood friend at this age makes me feel more vulnerable. All of us pay lip service to how important every day is. But I do have a greater appreciation for life, family, friends, and good health, at a level I didn't feel before. Paul lived life fully. He had been in semi-retirement mode for a while; he loved to watch old Westerns or war movies, play on his computer, or go flying. He took time with family and friends, and he used the good dishes. He had been doing for years what you are writing about. Gerry and I recently went out for lunch together to the same restaurant that the three of us used to go to. It's never going to be the same."

"Losing Paul makes me feel my mortality," Gerry admitted. "Our friendship was based on common interests, unspoken trust, and caring. With Paul gone, it's like missing the instrument in the orchestra that lightens up the piece. Sometimes I'll be in a restaurant and see three older men, maybe in their eighties, having

Every day I sing a song from my childhood like "London Bridge" or "Twinkle, Twinkle, Little Star."

Candice, marketing consultant

lunch together. It makes me feel sad that it won't be happening for the three of us."

But it is happening for Mary Thomas, 86, and her four eighty-something girlfriends from university days. For the past 20 years she's been lunching with "the girls" once a month. "All of us graduated from the University of Toronto on the same day 62 years ago. Of the five of us, three are widows and two never married. We just sit in the restaurant for hours and talk about everything. We rely on and accept each other. I do believe that friendship is the most important thing."

At 7:00 on every morning during the week, you'll find Bernie Younder, 58, on the telephone with his buddy John. "We've been calling each other at 7 a.m. for over 20 years. Sometimes we say three words to each other; other times we may speak for half an hour. We talk about everything without fear. John is an anchor, a sounding board for me. While we don't always agree, he is always there. He knows all my skeletons and I know his." John and Bernie reconnected in their mid-thirties after losing track of each other, and though they can go for weeks without seeing each other, they do speak every morning. "I was an only child," Bernie said, "so this relationship is very special to me. John is better than having a brother: I don't have to lend him my socks!"

Friendship. A magic connection that takes root and endures. Even with some neglect, there are usually enough sparks to keep the embers of that relationship warm. An e-mail or phone call may be enough to regularly stoke it, and a face-to-face get-together can restore the crackling fire. I am thankful that my best friend Linda lives only seven minutes away from me in Toronto. I am also fortunate to have a long-distance best friend, whom I e-mail weekly. Time and distance may slow down the pulse of our relationship, but when Sharon and I see each other, we swallow up the miles and hug with joy and laughter. Deep friendships have no boundaries. These are the friends who mourn with you, fly out for your wedding, or make the best dates when you are alone

I always stop and smell flowers any time I'm walking outside.
Ruth, physician

on New Year's. Cheerleaders, chauffeurs, and surrogate parents—best friends are there for each other. They are the joy in everyday life!

SOUP AND A HUG

Delicious. My spoon searched the bottom of the pot for one more tasty drop of Pat Bartlett-Richards' "sweep the fridge" soup. Appropriately named by her soulmate, George, to describe how Pat finds the ingredients, this soup is just one of the gifts she generously gives to those in need.

"George and I discovered a person in this apartment building who really needed soup and a hug," Pat explained. "One of the skills of giving is really listening. When you really listen to people's stories, you can hear what they need."

Every week, Pat, who knows what it feels like to be hungry, finds someone in her building who needs her special brand of nurturing. Born in northern Ontario and the eldest of seven children, Pat moved from town to town, sometimes "farmed out" to relatives and family friends. "We moved so much I never completed a full school year in any one school," she said. "We were poor, so at times there was not enough food, but my mother did teach me how to make soup."

At 16, Pat hitchhiked to Toronto and secured a job as a junior in a bank. With night school and university banking courses she propelled her way to management level. "Customer Service with Love" became her philosophy. Her compassion was evident; clients were invited to call her at home if there was an emergency. One Sunday she got a frantic call from a client's wife. In between sobs, she told Pat that their son had been in a car accident in Vancouver and was in a coma. She couldn't reach her husband, who was travelling in Europe. The mother needed to be with her son, but had no money. Pat calmly arranged everything: money, limousine

I eat a bag of potato chips every day.

Joanne, receptionist

to the airport, first-class airline ticket and hotel on Pat's account, and taxi service to and from the hospital. Pat eventually located the woman's husband, who immediately flew to Vancouver to be with his wife and son.

After her retirement a few years ago, Pat's humanitarian nature moved in a new direction. She became a talented artist, creating innovative abstracts by "marrying" paper and paint, wood and plastics, jewels and thread, cloth and glitter. Each unique piece tells a story from her life experiences and her travels through Canada, the United States, and the Far East. Net proceeds from the sale of her art assist charities in Canada, Nepal, and India. Her art is featured in the Rotary's TRAILS Lodge, which is dedicated to helping young people between the ages of 12 and 17 become the best that they can be.

"Giving," believes Pat, "is living with your heart, not your head. When you live in your heart, a warmth envelops you and everyone around you. I feel so joyous about life. I've been given many gifts—spiritual gifts, material gifts, the gift of health. I have a life full of presents every day. When you feel so happy and blessed, you've just got to give it back to help others."

A group of retired doctors in San Mateo, California, are "living with their hearts" by generously volunteering their time to provide health care to the poor. The Samaritan House Clinic began eight years ago as a one-room operation to help the homeless and the poor—anyone unable to afford health insurance. Today the clinic helps between 500 and 600 patients a month, and is staffed by 81 volunteers, many of whom are retired. Of the 27 physicians, 19 are retired. While a 70-year-old cardiologist may be "too old" to perform surgery in a hospital, his knowledge, dedication, and skills are invaluable here. The local hospital supports the endeavours of the clinic by providing free MRIs, CAT scans, and laboratory services. All drugs and medical supplies are donated. It is hard to tell who benefits the most—the patients or the doctors. The patients are so thankful for this service, and the

I take free samples of anything at gourmet food shops.
                                        Susan, receptionist

doctors are equally grateful that they can still contribute to a community that desperately needs help.

Another incentive for giving is that it may help you live longer. Anyone who has ladled soup for the homeless or sorted donated toys for needy children at Christmas returns home with a warm heart and a boost to their immune system. According to scientific studies, there is a physiological response called "helper's high" that releases brain chemicals known to decrease the stress response. This feel-good factor counteracts negative stress, which is a major factor in disease.

"My philosophy is to give without expecting to receive," said "Arctic" Joe Womersley. Once, before leaving for a holiday in Cuba, he packed his suitcase with extra shirts and running shoes to give away to kids and adults. "I had two shirts, almost new, and was looking for someone to give them to. I found a gardener who was working around the hotel and said, 'Here's a gift for you.' His entire face lit up, which made me feel so good. The next day he handed me a bunch of roses for my companion, which he gave from the bottom of his heart. I was very touched."

Doreen and Ben Wicks received Canada's highest civilian award, the Order of Canada, for their devotion to humanitarian causes. Ben has been involved in many charitable projects, including the Born to Read book series, which he wrote and illustrated and which has helped 2 million children learn to read, write, and count. His newest passion is called I.Can foundation, which links Canadian children and teens with community organizations. "There are so many lost kids with poor self-esteem," he believes. "This program will help kids stay active and involved in their community."

Ben is also very proud of Doreen. "When the doctor told Doreen that she had ovarian cancer, she said without hesitating, 'Okay, whatever it is, let's get on with it, because in six weeks I have to be in Peru to open six more health clinics.' She was more concerned about helping others than herself. That's the kind of

I love spraying my favourite perfumes on my neck and shoulders.
                                        Grace, advertising executive

person she is." In 1989, *Reader's Digest* featured Doreen in an article entitled "The Extraordinary Mrs. Wicks." And she is *truly* extraordinary. As the founder of Global Ed-Med Supplies Canada Inc. (GEMS) she helps the sick and poor in 65 countries around the world, and was instrumental in sending 50,000 blankets to help Ethiopian refugees. Each year GEMS distributes almost $1.5 million worth of aid: Cancer-treating equipment to a hospital in Peru; bed linens, infant cribs, and baby food to a maternity clinic in Trinidad; medicine and dressings to a leper colony in Haiti. In 1991 GEMS was involved in the Brazil Resettlement Program, moving desperately poor people to a vacant American Air Force base. Health groups were trained to care for those in the community, which has since grown from 5000 to 25,000. In 1993 GEMS gave young orphans in Uganda new opportunities by teaching them specialized skills. In 1997 the Doreen Wicks Foundation was created and the CAN START program was established to give the youth of Canada the opportunity to acquire the skills needed to get into the workplace.

Ben devotes half of his time to fundraising and publicity for GEMS. "In my experience," he concluded, "I have found that the biggest cause of unhappiness in people comes from thinking too much about yourself and your own problems. The happiest people I know reach out and give to others." Ben and Doreen Wicks are joyful indeed!

TO LOVE AND BE LOVED

It was her face, her beautiful, radiant, calm, loving face. I couldn't stop looking at her as she gazed lovingly into his eyes, nodding thoughtfully as he spoke. I was a silent observer of this palpable passion at a *satsang*—a gathering of people to share the truth. Once a month people come from all over to the Chopra Center for Wellbeing in La Jolla, California, to listen and share music,

> *I love the feeling of movement through space—walking, biking, and dancing.*
>
> *David, actor*

poetry, and wisdom. At this particular *satsang*, Dr. Deepak Chopra invited Kenny Loggins, the very talented musician, and his wife, Julia, to speak about their love, which is now chronicled in their book, *The Unimaginable Life: Lessons Learned on the Path of Love*. Kenny and Julia spoke openly and courageously about their "rocking and rolling" relationship, and their transformation as they fully opened their hearts to each other. "Feel your life," Kenny urged. "Create a dialogue with yourself, then you can be open to love others."

After sharing the most powerful expressions of their love, they encouraged questions from the audience. "What if you love someone who's not available?" someone asked. "Why are you attracting that in your life?" was the reply from the couple, who believe that we are mirrors of each other. And if we are simply mirrors of each other, it follows that what we feel we are missing is really about ourselves. If the level of intimacy in your relationship is not enough, Kenny and Julia explained, ask yourself, "Am I capable of giving more—of opening up?" If honesty and truth are issues, is it that I am not honest with myself? Everything starts with a psychologically healthy self."

Healthy individuals love without anxiety. The relationship continues to flourish with growing intimacy, honesty, and self-expression. They can be who they are in a couple, be spontaneous, and drop their defences. Healthy couples are cheerleaders for each other, eager for the growth of the other, showing respect for each other's individuality and unique personality. Healthy couplehood doesn't mean constant bliss. Happy couples can fight and argue. They know how to resolve their disagreements without causing emotional distance. They are in tune with one another, soothing and reassuring each other. In contrast, couples with marital discord attack each other during arguments, escalating into a downward spiral of blame, name-calling, and animosity. Healthy love is not suffocating, controlling, or needy. A relationship is not diminished by healthy selfishness, for we all need

Each day I honour the memory of my two beloved cats by visiting their gravesite in my backyard.

Ross, lawyer

to live our lives independently. Love needs regular consistent nurturing through attention, touch, and the spoken word. Love doesn't have to be demonstrated in big actions; rather, the small, ordinary, everyday moments are the most meaningful ones. This requires, first, the desire to please the other person. Real love endures beyond the frenzied "rip your clothes off" stage, eventually developing into an intimate, genuine, deep, caring, and loving friendship.

In my almost 23 years as a chiropractor, I have learned much about life and love from thousands of patients. Someone's face or eyes, or the words they choose, can tell me a great deal about the state of their relationship. I am not a psychotherapist; I work on muscles and joints, not on hearts. However, my openness about life allows patients to share their feelings on just about everything. Catherine has been married for ten years to Rick, "her best friend." Her eyes sparkled with affection as she described some of the ingredients for their happy relationship. "Our three kids are extremely important to us, but our relationship is a priority, too. We sometimes take vacations without them to rekindle our passion. Though we work different hours, we both work downtown. Rick waits for me to finish work so we can drive home together to catch up on each other's day. It's the little things we do for each other. Last year I was taking courses on Saturday, our usual chore day. Without saying anything, Rick took over the Saturday errands and chores so that we could have Sunday together. I always want to look my best for him. Even when I was in bed with the chicken pox, feeling lousy, I showered, brushed my teeth, and put on fresh lounge wear before Rick came home. For me, love cannot be learned from a book. It is a deep affection for a person that motivates me to behave lovingly."

Another couple, "Martha and George," have an enviable relationship after 11 years of marriage. "We have three children— ages five, eight, and ten—a dog, and a fish," Martha said with a laugh. "And a babysitter," she added. "Once a week we have a

As soon as I get home from the office, I take my shoes off and go barefoot.

Robert, financial officer

date night, to talk and spend time together. I call him at the office and we make a date on the telephone. I'll meet him at a restaurant or a theatre. Sometimes I won't be wearing any underwear, and I'll tell him so. That bothers him for the whole evening. If I *am* wearing underwear, I'll slip them off under the table and give them to him at dinner, in anticipation of what's to come! We love to tease each other and speak openly about our love for each other. There is great respect between us; we say thank you all the time, for things big or small." Her advice? "Never ever forget to tell that person how much they mean to you."

Mory Baxter met Gerre on a blind date when he was just 17. Now 76 years old and married for 56 wonderful years to Gerre, Mory can vividly remember the first time he met her. "I'll never forget the moment. It was Saturday, December 7, 1940. We were going to a formal dance," he recalled. "Gerre, who was 18, came down the stairs wearing a strapless gown, her long, chestnut-brown hair dancing around her shoulders. I was speechless; she was so beautiful. I've been in love ever since."

So, what is love?

"It's difficult for me to describe," Mory answered. "Our love has the five Cs—constancy, caring, communication, consideration, and commitment. We are best friends, talk openly, and touch each other. I feel happy knowing that she's happy. And we laugh a lot. Love is a long-term mutual desire to please and support the other person. I'm the luckiest guy in the world to have found Gerre!"

And how does his bride feel?

"After 56 years of married life, we continue to take pride in the other's achievements, and warmth and pleasure in each other's company," Gerre says. "We have boundless respect for each other. Communication has been one of our 'musts,' so each day we sit either in front of a fire or outside in easy chairs, chatting about the events of the day. Mory is my best friend and knows my innermost thoughts. I'd always hoped to find a gentle, loving, interesting,

No matter how hectic my day has been, I relax as soon as I go for a walk by the lake with my dog.

Nancy, radio broadcaster

good-looking, tender, thoughtful man—and I did!" I think they kinda like each other, don't you?

In the movie *Good Will Hunting*, there is a scene in which Robin Williams, whose wife has died from cancer, tries to describe to Matt Damon what love is. Although I can't recall the exact words, he says something like, "You can't know what love is by reading a sonnet. Love is holding your best friend's hand and watching her gasp her last breath. You don't know what it's like to feel totally vulnerable, to be with someone who could level you with her eyes. When you wake up beside that person you feel truly happy. You have so much love that sitting with her in the hospital, holding her hand, you know that visiting hours are not meant for you. That is love. When you love someone more than you love yourself."

Touched

Her tiny hand reaches out to mine,
Grasping my finger for the first time.
Touch expresses a heartfelt connection,
Holding hands is the voice of love and affection.
"Will you be my friend?" a child asks one day.
Two children join hands, giggle and play.
And then we grow up, sweaty palms, hormones racing,
Holding hands and more, teen passion needs pacing.
A man and a woman, a spark, an advance,
Hand touches hand, lovers romance.
"I'm so sorry," I express to friends who grieve,
I offer my hand to someone bereaved.
There's nothing better if you're sick with a cold
Than chicken soup, and a hand to hold.
"It's icy, Mom, dear. Remember when you fell?
Take my hand and your cane, gotta keep you well."

Every morning I enjoy my favourite breakfast—shredded wheat with soy milk, a banana, cinnamon, and honey on top.

Sandra, writer

A loved one lies dying, their weak hands you hold,
Sitting and hoping, then their hands go cold.
That hand slips away and makes us cry,
The last time we touch, the hand says goodbye.

Stopped in my car at a crosswalk, I watched a teacher lead a group of small children across the street, two by two, holding hands. As I sat there, I remembered something that profoundly affected me eight years ago. During a relaxing massage, I mentioned to the therapist that my left shoulder was sore. While I lay on my back, the therapist, who was standing at the head of the table, put his hand in my hand and raised my arm over my head to stretch the joint. Suddenly I burst into tears, remembering when, as a child of about five, I would walk with my dad, my little hand raised up above my head to reach his hand. I realized that we never outgrow the need for a hand to hold.

When we were kids at the doctor's office, holding mom's hand was one way to get through the ordeal. And if you were Dr. Robert Salter's patient, you would definitely feel his compassion and caring. "Prior to surgery and just before my young patients would fall asleep, I would take their hand. They would close their eyes knowing that I cared about them and I'd be there to see them after the operation. Something is transferred from one person to another in human touch. Shaking hands, the touch of a hand, a hand on a shoulder, says that you care about that person." When was the last time someone held your hand, and what did it mean for you? Was it a gesture of love, comfort, or safety?

Eight years ago, my brother Steven held my hand tightly as we stood solemnly while my mother's casket was lowered into the ground beside my dad. His hand in mine meant more to me than anything he could have said. It was a moment frozen in time.

My hand is and will always be the most personal, powerful part of myself. Whether I touch a patient, shake someone's hand, or walk hand in hand with my sweetheart, my hands communicate

Every day I take the time to enjoy a fantasy—a unique, enriching image or scenario.

Dina, psychologist

every possible emotion and experience. And I am very sensitive to the touch of others. Recently, I met a kind esthetician, Mitra Javdani, who gave me a manicure with a gentle touch. I discovered that her caring nature extended beyond her work. Mitra volunteers with Canadian Mothercraft, helping disadvantaged women through all stages of their pregnancy. "I might take them to special agencies for free clothing and furniture or stay with them overnight in the hospital," she explained. "I stay as long as it takes for them to deliver the baby. I hold their hand, massage them, comfort them, anything to help them relax. These women are immigrants, alone in this country. I know that I make a difference in their lives by just being there beside them. I feel privileged just to hold their hand and make them feel taken care of."

Life can be joyful in its simplicity. A spontaneous hug can be the best gift. Silently reaching over and taking your partner's hand while walking or in a darkened movie theatre conveys a message of love and caring. When I asked John Walsh, one of my patients, what small thing brings joy to his life, he told me something very poignant. "My dear wife of over 50 years had a stroke. I massage my wife's legs to make her feel good, which makes me feel good." Such a simple, caring gesture—a gift of touch. Touch is that heartfelt energy connection we give to others.

A NEW LIFE—GIVING TO OUR FUTURE

For most of you, December 9, 1999, was probably just another day on the calendar. But for the Dembe family, it was a day to rejoice, for we were blessed with the birth of Noah Brendon Dembe, son of Julie and Michael Dembe. Noah is the first grandson for my brother Steven, and his wife, Cheryl. With one giant push for mankind, our family grew just a little, and I became a great-aunt for the second time.

> I enjoy my morning ritual of a 15-minute hot shower and scrub with a hot cotton washcloth.
>
> *Charlotte, artist*

I attended Noah's bris, the circumcision ritual performed by a doctor (mohel) eight days after a Jewish boy is born. In a poignant ceremony at Julie and Michael's home, we welcomed this new life into our hearts. Our joy was palpable as we joined together in a lovely traditional way. Four members of our family held the *tallit* or prayer shawl, over Michael, Julie, and the baby. The others touched either an edge of the fabric or the shoulder of someone who was touching the *tallit*, so that we were all connected to each other. A Jewish educator from our synagogue then recited the following: "This *tallit* symbolizes the shelter of the loving home that Noah has been born into. Michael and Julie, you will provide the love and sustenance that Noah will need to grow. But as the *tallit* is open on all four sides, so all of you here also have a role to play, to help Noah grow, learn, and thrive. And so, I ask each person to give this baby a blessing. You may wish him a life of love and friendship, or courage to face his sorrows, or the blessing of good health." In turn, as we stood together in this circle of love around the baby, we offered our dreams and wishes for Noah as he began his life journey.

Our wish list for Noah included a curiosity for learning and a love of books; lasting friendships; that he become a decent and ethical person, kind and honest, with integrity and character; that he know the difference between right and wrong; that he not just do well, but do good; tenacity in pursuing his goals and passions; openness to adventure; the ability to adapt to life's challenges; a strong sense of family, caring, and compassion for others; the ability to laugh and be joyful; the wisdom to listen to his inner voice; flexibility with the ideas of others; health and wellness; that he love and be loved.

As I gazed at this helpless infant, my heart filled with hope. Children are a gift. They radiate innocence and purity in a sometimes jaded world. They bring adventure to a new day as they discover life with a fresh, whimsical spirit. With hope in their hearts, love in their touch, and trust in their eyes, they look to

I love sweating when I exercise.

Norm, teacher

adults for safety and love; we look to them for our tomorrows. They are our future. Though each of us has a unique life situation—some have children, some don't; some have families while in their twenties and others much later—children are a common thread linking all our stories: a thread of hope for the future.

What our children and grandchildren have depends on what *we give them.* What should we do to ensure a bright future for our children? What values must we teach them to help them on their path through life? How can we mentor them so they'll grow into mature, caring human beings? What gifts will give them a sense of history, tradition, and lasting memories?

Naturally, Great-Aunt Elaine only wants good things to happen in Tovah's and Noah's lives, but to be human is to experience both laughter and tears. No one lives happily ever after. When we are 50 or 60, we can look back and still remember how much the scraped knees and the lost loves hurt us. Yet they were as necessary to shape our lives as the home runs and the A in geography. With consistent, loving care, we can help children develop strategies to cope with challenges. It is not surprising that research shows that what we learn in the first years lasts forever.

What gifts can we give our children that they'll take into the future? The late Charlotte Klein, mother of Isaac, 16, Yael, 11, and David, 6, offers these thoughts: "Children need to be nurtured and loved from the minute they are born. When parents respect their children, children learn how to respect them back. Give them an appreciation of nature, a beautiful sunset. Show them a bird that has hurt itself and needs care, which is God's scheme of things. Faith is so important. A belief system provides a child with an anchor. All children need boundaries that teach them what their parents expect. Parameters give children a stronger foundation."

When Charlotte finished speaking, her son Isaac shared his thoughts: "My parents do so much to make me feel loved."

"Like what?" I asked.

I hold and hug my dog.

Sasha, age 13

"When I was in grade six, I had trouble reading Hebrew. My mom would wake up very early before school and help me with my Hebrew, so I could catch up to the other students in my class."

Isaac then mentioned a small loving gesture (that I also remember from my childhood!) that means a lot to him. "My mom holds my forehead whenever I get sick."

Danny Klein, father of Sasha, 13, says, "First, we must love our children. Then it is a matter of educating them, setting boundaries, and being a positive role model. What you do gives them a sense of dignity, self-respect, and confidence, then sets them on the road, giving them a nudge in the right direction. It is hard to know the right thing to do. Do I impart all of my values, or just some of them? Sasha believes in God and I don't. I am not going to lie to her about it. I let her know how I feel, and I respect her viewpoint. It is important to have a dialogue with her in an honest way, respecting her as an equal, even though I am her parent."

I asked Jennifer Glossop, editor and grandmother-in-waiting, what she hopes to pass down to her grandchildren: "I want to give them a love of books and the joy of learning. I remember my parents reading the Narnia books to me when I was young. I'm an only child, so books were my friends. I loved to disappear inside a book like *The Black Stallion*. Books were always a special gift at Christmas and on my birthday."

"I learned how to be patient and reflective from my father, who was very wise," said a judge. "I hope I have passed these qualities on to my children." An incident with his father in high school changed the course of his life. "I had a summer job as a radio announcer. When I was offered a full-time job, I went to my mother first and told her I wasn't going to university. She almost fainted, as both my parents had high hopes for me to further my education. So I went to my dad and said, 'I was offered this very good job with a good salary and I don't want to go to university.' My father sat there thoughtfully for several moments, then said, 'Son, radio broadcasting is going to be a very big industry.

I try to be friendly with everybody (except my brothers).

Yael, age 11

If you went to university, you'd be the best broadcaster in Canada. Why don't you go to university first, then go into broadcasting?' So, I did. I stood at the top of my class and decided to go to law school instead. My father's calm wisdom taught me to sit back and reflect on things first before making a decision or giving a quick answer. We need to teach this to our children."

"The best gift you can give to children is a happy memory," believes artist Doris McCarthy, 89. "Memories last, and they influence children for the rest of their lives."

"I hope I have passed many gifts onto my son Paul," said Pearl Cassel, 68, speaker, author, and family counsellor. "Good health, enjoyment and creativity, someone to love him (wife, children, and friends), to feel dignity and respect for himself and others, a sense of humour and not to take himself too seriously."

Barbara Burrows, psychotherapist and director of Barbara Burrows Parenting, explains what a child needs to ensure an emotionally healthy future: "Children need a reliable, dependable, trustworthy, and committed caregiver (usually the mother and father, but a trusted nanny can also suffice—as long as the relationship is not severed) with whom they can identify. This consistent, loving person provides a relationship. It is in the context of this relationship that the child develops a conscience, values, a sense of responsibility, and a desire to learn. So we need to look after a child's emotional needs when they're young, then let them go emotionally as the child develops over many years to an independent emotional state."

What else can we give to our future generation? Each one of us, with or without children, is concerned with passing on certain values to the next generation, making sure that the good things of civilization—democracy, justice, integrity—are retained and nourished in the future. How do we pass these values along? We might begin by remembering that values never change. Children still have to learn the importance of respecting others, the role of generosity and honesty, the need for patience and compassion.

I love waking up when I feel like it.

David, age six

They also need to be true to themselves. When Bernie Klein spoke at his youngest son's bar mitzvah, he concluded his speech with his favourite saying from the Jewish Book of Ethics: "Jordan, this is a saying that describes the type of person I aspire to become and hope you will become:

> *If I am not for myself, who will be for me?*
> *And if I am only for myself, what am I?*
> *And if not now, when?"*

To me this says it all. We could not hope for anything better for our children, our future.

Noah slept peacefully, unaware of my thoughts on his future. While I will gladly leave the parenting to Julie and Michael, Great-Aunt Elaine has much to share with Noah and Tovah. It will be exciting to watch them grow up. There are family stories to share, rituals and traditions to teach, and memories to enjoy. My brother Steven is writing a history of our father, Harry, so that his contributions and life journey will not be lost. While Noah and Tovah, and their children, will never know Harry, photographs, medals, and the retelling of his fascinating life will paint a portrait they can carry into the future. As we approach mid-life, we need to remember how much we can influence the younger ones who are waiting in the wings, full of hope and enthusiasm. Like a runner halfway through the marathon of life, we need to jog back a ways to help those who are only just beginning. At best, we can share what we have learned so far—the upcoming hills, the twists and turns in the road. It is our truth as we see it. We can only tell them what it's like up ahead, but they have to run every step of the way themselves, never alone, but on their own.

I dream of a hole-in-one.

Jordan, age 15

CELEBRATING

CELEBRATING YOUR LIFE STORY

When you really listen to the way people tell their life story—the words they choose and how they explain where they are and what they've been through, you can begin to understand the depths of their lives. While researching two books and listening to the life stories of 82 exceptional older adults I learned that we can be joyful no matter what has happened to us. How we determine the meaning of our lives depends on how we perceive it. And most importantly, telling and retelling our life story to others helps us to shape its meaning.

In his book *How Good Do We Have to Be?* Rabbi Harold Kushner shares the wisdom of a colleague who taught him the secret of composing a eulogy: "Every human being's life is a story, a unique story that nobody ever lived before and no one will ever live again. What we want to know about a book or a movie is not how long it is, but how good it is, and we can learn to think of life in the same way. If life is a story, then we understand it better as we get closer to the end. Only then can we understand the real significance of something that happened back in chapter three or four."

The wise individuals I met are living near the end of their story. They can stand at the top of the mountain, look back at the path they chose, and somehow make sense of it. I'm not there yet, and I admit it would be tempting to skip over the parts of my life that were painful. But even at mid-life, I can stand near the top of a big hill, look back, and understand that I had to live through those parts of my story to pave the way for the joy that has followed. Mom was right when she told us to respect our elders. Here are some key things I learned from the sages:

I smile.

Judith, R.N. receptionist

1. Embrace a sense of gratitude for the privilege of just being alive— celebrate both the joys and the struggles.
2. Try to discover meaning and purpose in all aspects of living.
3. Trust in the universe, and enjoy how that trust connects you to all living things.
4. Make peace with the world; try to avoid resentment, anger, and fear, even when you are going through painful periods of your life.
5. Don't rush through life. Too often our life stories are but a quick read to the end. *Tempus fugit.* Before we know it, the credits are rolling.

"I am grateful for everything that's happened—good and bad things," expressed Don Wright, 90. "Grateful for the bad things, as they taught me some damn good lessons!" "Learning to love and learning to let go and trust," Doris McCarthy, 89, advised me, "is what life is all about. Change is going to happen, and it happens far more often than you welcome it. Trust that the future is going to be as good as the past, if not better. Life is not a tour or a cruise. You make your own life for better or worse, as you learn to love."

Dr. Dan Baker is the clinical director of the Life Enhancement Center at Canyon Ranch, which offers week-long programs for people who want to make changes in their lives. "We need to create better life stories," Dr. Baker believes. "Ask yourself: Do my life stories limit my vision, minimize my potential, create negative experiences, or devalue me? Or do they create new possibilities that inspire, grow, and stretch me? Do they provide passion and purpose, and represent my core values?" After working with over-achieving professionals for 14 years, he began to see that the same events in people's lives were interpreted in either constructive or destructive ways depending on that individual's perception of the event. "Too often we tell ourselves scary, fear-driven stories. Fear is so reactive, there is no room for choice in our life. What are the daily stories we tell ourselves about our health, relationships, and work?"

I read food recipes and imagine how they'll taste.
Shay, gourmet food store owner

Dr. Baker explained how he helped one executive alter his fear-driven belief that work had to be the most important thing in his life. "I gave this client a homework assignment: Spend two days volunteering at a pediatric-oncology ward," he said. Baker made the necessary arrangements. "I could have talked about life and death until I was blue in the face, but he had to gain that perspective for himself. He called me two months later and said, 'Now I understand. I have some serious issues involving work.'" The client began to spend more time with his family.

Most people, Baker says, are open and honest about life, until they need to be open and honest with themselves. Introspection takes courage, which is why he asks clients to think about their lives as if they were on their deathbed. "People on their deathbed look back on life with a special perspective. They discard trivia and focus on what matters most: on relationships, on 'defining moments'—those critical choices that lead us down one path or another."

And what of Dr. Baker's own story? How does he perceive and interpret his life lessons, particularly the "bad" parts. "I don't call them bad parts," he said. "Pain teaches me to grow in my resilience, my understanding, and my wisdom. A painful experience is a profound lesson. The real question is what am I to learn? Is it patience, tolerance, appreciation for what I have had?" Dr. Baker has endured the death of an infant son and yet he explains his loss in an empowering way. "My son left me a legacy. He taught me that life is fragile and precious, and that relationships with other human beings are the most important thing in life. Sometimes I demand that the world be the way I want it to be." He joked, "Since I have not yet been conferred with the credentials of God, I don't have the power to make it happen."

Think about your life story so far. Do you value, appreciate, and celebrate everything you've learned? If I asked you to tell me your best life stories, would you eliminate the painful ones? We need to understand that all of our experiences are life's "best stories."

Every night after prayers and a story, my three-year-old and I have a chat about her day.

Susan, human resources director

Only when we realize that we can be happy no matter what has happened in our lives, Dr. Baker believes, can we, "check out with few regrets. We can say 'I have learned greatly. I have been a good student and maybe, if I've been fortunate, a good teacher.'"

LUCKY

I confess to glancing at the obituaries in the newspaper. A cursory scan of the names takes maybe 20 or 30 seconds; I rarely stop to read the death notices. But for some reason on August 24, 1999, I did stop. Although I did not know him at all, I was drawn to one man's name and began reading this brief summary of his life.

> Cassel, Sidney On August 23, 1999, at Sunnybrook Health Science Centre of a brain tumour, age 66. Though it had appeared that he would have many more tennis tournaments to win, golf games to play, and bizarre results to achieve at the bridge table, he greeted his sudden illness with contentment and gratitude for his life. Indeed he played hard, planned land deals, and consulted to his son's business right up until his final week. In accordance with his wishes, his remains have been donated to science and there shall be no ceremony. In Sid's memory, it is suggested that his best jokes be passed along. Donations in lieu of flowers will be accepted towards a public bench he felt was badly needed at a bus stop near his last home.

I was so touched and curious to learn more about the life of this man that I contacted Pearl, his widow, whose telephone number was listed at the bottom of the notice. Within moments of introducing myself, I knew that the universe had purposely connected us. Pearl and I share a similar philosophy: "People are put on our

Each morning I do a couple hundred sit-ups, which makes me feel great.

Michael, lawyer

path whom we can help or who can help us. You just have to remain open to the possibilities," she believes. We agreed to meet at my office for an interview.

"My son Paul composed that obituary," Pearl began, "and if you knew Sidney, you'd be even more touched by what he wrote. Sid played the game of life. He loved golf, bridge, tennis, Scrabble, any sport, and he played as much, as hard, as long, and as well as he could. He was a risk-taker, opinionated, self-sufficient, a good marriage partner, a good business partner, an emotional and spiritual partner, and a very generous and loving person. He was creative, artistic, and loved to paint. He laughed easily and told jokes all the time." Pearl handed me a picture of Sidney and said, "He was a dandy dresser, always buying expensive clothes and sports equipment— definitely living out of the top drawer! After 37 years of marriage, we still walked through life hand in hand, not one in front or one behind, just together." Pearl then reached into her purse and pulled out a piece of paper. "Would you like to hear Sidney's last words?" He dictated them to me from his hospital bed."

> I am ready to leave. I don't want to think any more. I feel at peace with the world. My debts are paid. I ask my son Paul and Pearl to forgive me. I have no resentments. Nobody did me any harm. I am ready to die. I accept this situation. My life has been very lucky. I've been the luckiest man alive and still am.

"My son came into the hospital room and, with Sid looking on, I read his last words," said Pearl. The next morning Paul came back to the hospital with three silver rings with the word "Lucky" engraved on them. He gave one to his father, one to me, and kept one for himself." In a celebratory gesture, the three of them clicked their rings together and proclaimed, "We are the lucky Cassels!" Pearl laughed. "Sid was so thrilled he could hardly speak." It was Sidney's wish that his organs be donated to help others. Five

> I sit down at the breakfast table with a view that looks out over a ravine, reading my newspaper while eating cereal with fresh berries, followed by a cup of strong black coffee.
>
> Rona, magazine editor

people benefited from that final unselfish act. Although I never met Sidney Cassel, I sense that many were lucky to know this special man who definitely used the good dishes throughout his life.

TRUSTING THE UNIVERSE

I have always been fascinated by the inexplicable—the "meaningful coincidences"—that happen to all of us. I regularly consult with my astrologer, Sharon Holesh, who guides me on planetary matters, and two psychics have astonished me with extraordinary readings. I feel intuitively that I am being directed in some way, on a path that is naturally right for me. In my gut, I sense a purpose and meaning for just about everything that happens to me—the good stuff and the painful. Even when I am sad or worried, or perhaps disappointed, I am able to recover more quickly than I used to. With the help of my inner voice, which is more interested in "What can I learn from this?" than "Why did this happen?" I bounce back to my happy, joyful self again. I have heard it said that "Our failures are God's way of redirecting us." This perspective allows me to trust that the universe is unfolding as it should.

I never feel alone or isolated in the world, because I am always connected to the deeper, richer, and more joyful aspects of life. A chance meeting, a switchboard operator that mistakenly connects me to someone I should meet, a cancelled appointment that turns out to be beneficial, someone mentioning the very thing I've been looking for, a casual remark that changes my perception, a book that falls off the shelf—all of these become adventures. I tell myself that the universe is speaking, and it's as though my life is a big treasure hunt leading me on a very exciting journey.

Carl Jung was so intrigued by coincidences that he coined the term "synchronicity." What makes these "meaningful arrangements"

I find humour in the smallest things, like calling myself a "professional petroleum flow coordinator."

Tony, PPFC (gas station attendant)

(Jung's term) so puzzling is that they that have no apparent causal link, suggesting some hidden force that influences our time and space. Here are some coincidences or synchronous events that I can't dismiss as luck or chance.

- In the 1970s (before I became a chiropractor) I began manufacturing and distributing hand-crocheted fashion accessories (rings, chokers, snoods, and belts) in Hamilton. The items were made by 12 skilled women who worked out of their own homes. One morning, I decided it was time to crack the market in Toronto. I hadn't made any appointments with buyers beforehand, and I prayed in the car that someone would give me a chance. I drove into the "big city" with positive expectations. My very first call was to a fancy hair salon with a boutique in its reception area. Believe it or not, the fashion editor of the *Toronto Star* happened to be there having her hair done. She noticed the jewellery, loved my entrepreneurial spirit, and wrote a full-page article for the cover of what used to be called the Women's section, instantly launching my career.
- After my mother died, my brother Steven found an old photographic slide of the house in which we grew up and enlarged it as a surprise to cheer me up. As we studied the beautiful photograph, we were stunned and thrilled to see our dear mother in the picture, standing in a window of the house. She had not been visible until the slide was enlarged. I think this may have been my mother's way of sending us a comforting message that she was okay.
- A few years ago, I was about to leave on a trip, having made arrangements with my basement tenant to feed my cherished, 17-year-old cat while I was away. My friend David was taking me to the airport. He drove up, stopped his car, and came into my house to help with the suitcases. But when we were ready to leave, the car wouldn't start. After many

I allow my senses to intoxicate me through beautiful music, nature, or people.

William, financial analyst

failed attempts, we decided to take my car instead. While we transferred the suitcases from his car to mine, a car screeched to a stop in front of us. My tenant jumped out, relieved to find that I had not yet left. She had lost her house keys, and would have been locked out for the weekend. I gave her my spare key, and then David's car started immediately. Had his car started on the first try, and had we not been delayed, my tenant would have missed me, and both she and my cat would have been marooned.

Here are some more thoughts on trusting: From Grace Irwin, 92, "So much comes from my belief that God has a purpose for me—a plan. I trust the universe." Composer-musician Phil Nimmons, 76, feels there are some unexplained miracles of life. "I wrote a piece of classical music when I was just a teenager that was almost note for note the same as one composed many years later by a famous composer. Maybe everything is connected."

Mary Bourn, 91, feels she was saved by a guardian angel who appeared at just the right time when she was desperate for help. "In 1931, when I was 22, there was a terrible snowstorm. I'll never forget it. I missed the train going to Lindsay and had to walk the rest of the way home—thirteen miles alone, out in the country. I decided to walk along the railway tracks, as the roads were impassable." The howling winds whipped across the flat farmer's fields and blew snow in her face. With no hat to keep her head warm, Mary felt cold and increasingly tired as she walked, feet plunging into the deep snow. As darkness approached, Mary plodded along, chilled to the bone and feeling more weary with each step. "Suddenly I noticed a figure in the distance. A farmer was coming towards me with a big jar of milk. I told him I was very thirsty, so he stopped and gave me a drink. That milk was like manna in the desert. Even though I was only halfway there, I had enough strength after that to continue, and I eventually made it home safe."

Every morning I concoct a healthy vegetable cocktail in my juicer.
Sharon, astrologer

While discussing the tragic loss of his seven-year-old son after heart surgery, Joseph Sorbara revealed that he believes he was warned about it two years earlier. "I began practising law in 1970," Joseph explained, "and one of my first clients off the street was a man who wanted me to sue Toronto's Hospital for Sick Children. Apparently his son had died after heart surgery. I spent several hours with this client taking down all the details. I then spent the afternoon looking up his son's name and checking records. The hospital had no record of that patient ever being admitted. The phone number and address of the client did not exist. I never heard from him again. That bizarre occurrence somehow helped me to cope with my loss."

After her grandson, Adam, died from sudden infant death syndrome, Darlene Lamb found herself struggling with depression. A friend invited her to a cottage on a lake, hoping that the tranquil setting would help her heal. Darlene, who grew up on a farm in Saskatchewan, always loved watching clouds. "In the winter, I used to lie on my back making snow angels, looking up at the big sky," she recalled. One evening at the lake, as she was watching the sunset with her camera and tripod in tow, she looked up and saw a cloud in the shape of an angel carrying a gift. She quickly took a picture. "Within moments, the wind had dispersed the clouds and the angel was gone."

Then Darlene's daughter, Adam's mother, saw the photograph. "Oh my God!" she exclaimed. "It's an angel carrying a baby!" Suddenly Darlene realized that this was the solace she had been looking for. "I thought, if Adam's soul can so quickly move on to his next adventure, surely I can, with the same strength, move on with my life somehow." Though Darlene took the photo, she doesn't think of it as hers. "It's for everyone, because Adam was a gift." She has since entitled it "The Gift" and had the photo made into beautiful greeting cards, which I send out to bereaved patients. Deeply affected by the image, Darlene says that it taught her "not to give up on life but to give it up to a higher power."

Every morning I feed birdseed to about 20 or 30 hungry goldfinches.
Linda, artist

An angel doesn't have to sport wings. An angel can come in the form of the truck driver who rescued my assistant, Dina, on the highway after her van was sideswiped and flipped over. He helped her climb out of the back door of the badly damaged vehicle, gave her his jacket, retrieved her glasses and mail, called her husband, called me at home, and then waited with her until an ambulance arrived.

Human kindness shows itself often. You may appreciate it as common decency or as ethereal currents helping you on your path. But it's uplifting to uncover the subtle hints of meaning in life that we may otherwise pass by. I knew that Gerda Sippert had ethereal energy after a conversation we had at the hairdresser. "I completely trust the universe," she said. "I meditate, pray for guidance and protection, and write in a journal. Every day I visualize exactly what I want out of my life—physically, mentally, and spiritually. Then I go about my day. This gives me comfort and joy."

My friend Wendy Harris also finds comfort in her surroundings. "I look for meaning everywhere, always searching for the answers to life's questions." Wendy attributes her spirituality to four key influences: her father, who she calls a "spiritual mentor" and who taught her to be optimistic and focused on the present; AA meetings (attended with an alcoholic friend), which she found powerful and extremely moving; Deepak Chopra, whose life-altering books resonate in her heart; and her mother, who Wendy says has seen spirits. "Ask for what you want, then let that desire or intention go and live your life positively. Stop wondering when or how your desires will be fulfilled. I get so many gifts back. I can have a spiritual connection while chatting with people at the office. When you are conscious of your life, you can stay positive, even in the face of negative people or difficult experiences. I treat people the way I want to be treated."

So where is the joy?

"Everywhere! I am so grateful for my life. When you trust the universe, it's like having an assistant who is helping you on your path."

I watch in awe as hummingbirds magically appear when I fill their feeder each morning.

Barry, cinematographer

GRATITUDE AND PRIVILEGE

About a dozen framed photographs of different men hang on the wall of Dr. Robert Salter's office. "These are my teachers," he explained, "my mentors. I am grateful for what they have given me, for the privilege of being taught by some of the world's leading medical educators. Sir Isaac Newton wrote, 'We see so far because we stand on the shoulders of giants.' These men are the giants in my life." Dr. Salter then handed me a copy of a convocation address that he delivered to new graduate doctors entitled "An Equation of Life for Health Professionals." In his speech, he explained seven privileges that these professionals had been given through no work of their own. He spoke of devoted parents; an above-average intelligence; the privilege of living in a free country; the gift of good health—physically and mentally; love, companionship, and the support of spouses; learned teachers; and the privilege of secure and ready employment. Dr. Salter's "Equation of Life" is for everyone. We are all the product of parents, teachers, friends, communities, and mentors who gladly take us by the hand and guide us on our path. A wise person once said, "Only we can do it, but we can't do it alone." We need to be conscious of, and thankful for, the casts of thousands who, over our lifetimes, help us in ways big and small.

The older I get, the more I understand this. When we were children, our parents taught us to say please and thank you. Then came the tedious task of writing thank-you notes for gifts, which in our house was *de rigueur*. I don't remember feeling particularly thankful as a teenager, probably because I was too busy fretting over the things I wanted and couldn't have. Now I recognize that most things in life are privileges, not rights. I am cognizant of the many kindnesses people do for me, from my neighbour Barbara, who looks after my house when I am away, to my invaluable assistant, Dina, who tends to me and our office with devotion and love.

I love the fresh-air smell of white sheets and towels when I bring them in from the clothesline.

Linda, artist

Dr. Deepak Chopra defined gratitude as "the acknowledgement that it is a privilege and a surprise just to exist." Just to exist! To be alive, to wake up in the morning and realize you're breathing, to be able to see, hear, smell, taste, and touch! And that is even before we get our (miraculous!) bodies out of bed and enjoy even more gifts, like hot water and soap, clothes, and food. How many people appreciate these wonders?

We can become smug, cocooned in our safe, predictable world, and often something must happen to make us feel grateful or remind us of the fragility of life. A funeral, a friend being diagnosed with cancer, a close call in a car, witnessing an accident—all have a way of yanking us out of our complacency. Often we say these words silently to ourselves: "There, but for the grace of God, go I." I've been told that my poem "Use the Good Dishes" has been read at several funerals, a sombre and fitting place to hear these words: "...all the day-to-day lessons we learn, be grateful for the rough ones, the pain and the tough ones, *everyone has their turn.*" The older adults I interviewed for this book understand this better than anyone, because the older we get, the more grateful we become. Imagine how grateful they must feel, since even at my age I feel blessed to enjoy great health and unbridled energy to do everything I want to do.

From Helen Gougeon, 76: "Every morning I wake up and say a grateful thank you that I made it to another day. The last thing I do at night is say a prayer of thanks for all of the wonderful things in my life. On my deathbed, I don't think there are going to be any regrets. I've had it all in spades and I am fully aware of my good fortune in having grown old with a positive attitude."

From Rabbi Bernard Baskin, 80: "I am grateful that I was born with good genes, that I had nurturing parents, that my life's work has been meaningful. I am lucky to have a fine mate, good health, and seven healthy grandchildren. You must take what life has given you, the hand you are dealt."

From Pearl Cassel, 78: "I wake up in the morning and thank my

I enjoy my evening walk in the country, with the darkness, the stars in the sky, and the silence.

George, *designer*

higher power for a good night. I say to myself, 'We're going to enjoy this day.' At night, I think over the events of the day and say, 'That was nice, meeting Elaine, or it was good to see that little child.' I am grateful for it all."

All of us have had thousands of happy, joyful memories and out-standing experiences in our lifetimes, and we can all think of things that make us angry or miserable. I am not suggesting that you bury those painful moments. Rather, try to recognize and be conscious of all the good in your life. In Chapter 4, Remembering, I recommend starting a happy memory book for this purpose. Rereading the joyful moments in your life will stimulate grati-tude. As I wrote in *Passionate Longevity*, my father taught me an old Yiddish saying: "If everyone hung their problems on a fence for everyone else to see, you'd end up taking your own problems back!" We all need to remember this. Look around and you will see that everyone's life has its measure of joy and difficulties. Happy, optimistic people appreciate and accept that fact. I feel so grateful and blessed for my life. Every day I think about the priv-ilege of being able to work in a profession I love, of the skill I've been given through my spoken and written words, of my health, family, love, and dear friends. I am also grateful for the lessons I've had to learn the hard way—the pain and the losses.

Life is a privilege, not to be taken for granted, and gratitude is a by-product of that discovery. And when you feel grateful, as Dr. Salter believes, "You will want to give something back in return for what you have been given."

MY HOME: THE EARTH

The world gave a party and the whole world showed up! As the clock struck midnight on New Year's Eve, 1999, wherever you lived—from Tonga to Toronto—planet Earth united in celebration to "firecracker in" the year 2000. And thanks to technology,

I love coming downstairs to the smell of freshly baked bread and tast-ing that first slice.

Brad, producer

humankind witnessed it all. Thousands of kilometres above the Earth, the world's television networks tied up nearly every available satellite to deliver monumental 24-hour coverage. Unlike most parties, you were expected to appear either fashionably late or early at this one, depending on the time on your watch. There I was on December 31, 1999, in my hotel room in Tucson, Arizona, television remote control in hand, flipping channels back and forth. CNN, PBS, and ABC tracked the arrival of the new year around the globe, from the remote Pacific island of Kiribati to the big cities of Moscow, London, New York, and Honolulu. And I didn't want to miss any of it.

I was invited to watch London celebrate, as the Queen lit a torch setting the Thames ablaze in a huge fireworks display below the capital's giant new Ferris wheel and the Millennium Dome hosted a party for 10,000. The Eiffel Tower in Paris was transformed into a spectacular sprinkler catapulting light in all directions. Fiery sea creatures, three storeys high, crossed Sydney's harbour, and as midnight arrived twenty tons of fireworks lit up the summer night. In Bethlehem, 2000 peace doves were released into the night sky. Laser projectors lit up the Giza pyramids as Egypt ushered in the new year with a sunset to sunrise electronic opera. Millions of revellers thronged Brandenburg Gate in Berlin to watch the pyramid of light show. In Rio de Janeiro, 3 million people dressed in white greeted the year 2000 on Cococabana beach by sending flowers and floating candles into the Atlantic Ocean. Choirs, traditional dances, prayers of peace, tribal parties—the world rejoiced as we heralded the new year across the globe.

I was transfixed in front of the television. Never before had I witnessed a single event that crossed all borders, countries, and continents. Regardless of nationality or cultural or religious beliefs, the entire planet was celebrating the year 2000. The Hebrew calendar might read 5760, but for that one 24-hour period it didn't matter; the world was one. As I watched 198 nations in harmony, my perception of the world changed. My mind was no longer

Every morning I have a chatty conversation with my silverbill finch and then I work in my studio.

Linda, artist

restricted by thoughts of my little home on the north side of a small street in the city of Toronto, province of Ontario, country of Canada, continent of North America. Instead, I realized that my home was Earth. I felt a global consciousness, and a connection to all human beings on Earth. The thought that humankind was a single community made me feel hopeful for the future. This universal celebration was a global thread that linked all of us through our shared hopes, fears, and joy, beyond all differences.

Then my mind began to create an even broader context of reality. If I now feel totally connected to Earth, with feet firmly rooted here on this planet, how must astronauts feel when viewing the entire planet from millions of miles away? Dr. Roberta Bondar, Canada's first woman in space, described how she felt the first time she looked back at Earth during the spaceship *Discovery's* January 1992 flight: "When I looked out and saw Earth...something comes to life for you, an incredible emotion. You realize that it's a total planet, not a megacity...not Quebec and the rest of Canada. You realize that we need all the resources of every culture." Oleg Makarov, a four-time cosmonaut aboard the Russian ship *Soyuz* in the 1970s, said, "When I turn off the light in my studio and trace my path home in the darkness, I will be aware that I am walking on a round planet hurtling around the sun at 62,000 miles an hour, turning at 1000 miles an hour at the equator, producing day and night. I will be aware of our sun as the centre of a solar system that is moving around the galaxy at more than 500,000 miles an hour, and of the whole galaxy itself hurtling in a direction unknown to me at an unimaginable speed through an ever-expanding universe populated with billions of other galaxies stretching to eternity." This is definitely the big picture!

We know how striking a sunrise or sunset can be. Astronaut Joseph Allen (*Columbia 5*, 1982) describes his unique vantage point: "Each sunrise and sunset lasts only a few seconds. But in that time you see at least eight different bands of colour come and go, from a brilliant red to the brightest and deepest blue. And you

I love getting a daily phone call from my two-year-old grandson, who recently learned which speed dial button to push to reach me.

Cris, manager

see 16 sunrises and sunsets during every day you're in space. No sunrise and sunset is ever the same."

How small does Earth look when you're in space? Buzz Aldrin (*Apollo 11*, 1969) describes Earth as "being so small I could blot it out of the universe simply by holding up my thumb." From James Irwin (*Apollo 15*, 1971): "The Earth reminded us of a Christmas tree ornament hanging in the blackness of Space. As we got farther and farther away it diminished in size. Finally it shrank to the size of a marble, the most beautiful marble you can imagine."

My sentiments of unity are expressed by astronaut John-David Bartoe (*Challenger 8*, 1985): "As I looked down, I saw a large river meandering slowly along for miles, passing from one country to another without stopping. I also saw huge forests extending across several borders. And I watched the extent of one ocean touch the shores of separate continents. Two words leaped to mind as I looked down on all this: commonalty and interdependence. We are one world." And it is this same feeling of oneness that Sultan Bin Salman al-Saud (*Discovery*, 1985) described as he noticed both borders and differences melt away among his fellow astronauts: "The first day or so we all pointed to our countries. The third or fourth day we were pointing to our continents. By the fifth day we were aware of only one Earth."

It is my hope and dream as only one human being on this Earth that all of us join in a universal consciousness to keep our planet beautiful, safe, and peaceful. An old Chinese proverb describes how one person can change the world:

If there is light in the soul,
There will be beauty in the person.
If there is beauty in the person,
There will be harmony in the house.
If there is harmony in the house,
There will be order in the nation.
If there is order in the nation,
There will be peace in the world.

When I get home from work, I unwind by listening to soft jazz music and sipping a glass of wine.

Helen, computer training

WHERE'S THE JOY?

The sky was still ribboned with dark clouds as I set out for an early morning run, surrounded by the cactus-studded foothills of Tucson, Arizona. With each passing moment, almost pulsing to the beat of my footsteps, the sky was preparing to herald a new day. I watched intently as the blackened silhouette of the nearby mountains slowly developed an orange blush. Golden-yellow streaks of light emerged through a pocket in the clouds. Suddenly a single rainbow-like arc of radiance was visible, casting a brush of gold across the width of the sky and painting the face of one mountain. I stopped running, too awestruck to continue. Though the other peaks were still cloaked in night's darkness, the entire surface of this mountain glowed like a golden fire. I looked up and down the road, hoping to find someone to share this experience with; there wasn't even a dog barking. Within minutes, dawn's unstoppable force of illumination streamed forth and my gold mountain disappeared. Desperate to express my euphoria after witnessing this beautiful sunrise, I looked up at the heavens, my voice jubilant, "Thank you, God, for this beautiful moment!" I continued on my run lighter in step, my heart bursting with joy.

A fragment in time, that is all, and then that joyful moment was gone. But now, far away from cactus plants and the mountains, I can still celebrate that gift with closed eyes and my memory. Although the moment was just a transient particle of time, it will endure. And that is what using the good dishes is all about. It is about delighting in the moments that don't last, in the joys that fade before our eyes—a sunrise, a wonderful laugh, a baby's smile, the surprise of a flower that blooms overnight, a hug from a loved one. Though I thought at the time, "If only I had my camera to capture this magnificent sunrise," we need to relish these moments now rather than wait for our camera, or until we have more time or money, or until we meet the right person to share it with, because then we miss out. These moments don't last forever. Or

I try to be kind to my wife every day.

Paul, entertainer

perhaps we are too rushed, too busy, too self-absorbed, or too unconscious to notice the life around us. We cannot stop time at our whim, until we finally get around to being a part of life. Too soon these moments are gone, and so are we. The late author Erma Bombeck wrote in a touching article, "If I Had My Life to Live Over," "There would have been more I love yous, more I'm sorrys, more I'm listenings, but mostly given another shot at life, I would seize every minute of it, look at it and really see it...try it on...live it...exhaust it...and never give that minute back until there was nothing left of it."

Pearl Cassel expressed these same thoughts in a most poetic fashion: "We have to embrace and respect each moment of life; every moment is a sparkle in time. We do this with our eyes open. To look is one thing: to really see what we look at is another. To understand what we are looking at is a part of wisdom, but to *live* with the knowledge of what we understand is real growth."

In the process of writing this book, I have met many people who live life with their eyes fully open. Dr. Dan Baker describes a typical joyful morning: "I use my senses. When I wake up in the morning, I feel my wife next to me and that brings me joy. Usually one of our dogs jumps up on the bed and licks my face. I live on a ten-acre property, and when I stand up and look out the window, I see the golden aura of the sun just behind the mountains, and I realize what an awesome phenomenon it is. I have a delicious breakfast and then I work out. I feel my body, and the energy and clarity from that nourishment. I don't turn on the radio or think about work during my drive to the office. The silence allows me to contemplate life, being quiet, calm, and appreciative. That is how I begin my day."

Four years ago, Henry Less and his seven-year-old daughter decided to transform every mealtime into a joyous celebration. "We now use the good dishes for every day. If you open our cutlery drawer, you'll see the good silver. Even if it's only breakfast, we set the table with silver salt and pepper shakers and cloth napkins. The

Every day there is a friend in my life.

Ruth, marketing director

milk is transferred from the carton into our fancy creamer and we drink orange juice from crystal goblets. When Monica and I are together, every meal is special."

From Pat Bartlett-Richards: "George and I set our kitchen table as if we're having the Queen for dinner. Fresh flowers adorn its centre and there are lit candles on either side. And we use the good dishes. If you can't enjoy a dinner at home in the same way as you do a $200 meal at a restaurant, something is lost in your life somewhere."

Dentist Dr. Janet Tamo has been using the good dishes since childhood. "I remember my mother taking me to buy new shoes when I was five. I always had to wear the new shoes home; I never wanted them to be put back in the box. If Mom bought me a new outfit, I had to wear it that day. I'm not into saving stuff. I live for the moment. My husband and I aren't waiting for retirement to travel or have fun. I'm into friend-and-fun-accumulating now, not wealth-accumulating for some time in the future."

When Ben Wicks hosted his own television show, he interviewed many famous people, from world leaders to movie stars. Yet when I asked him to name someone he knew who led a happy and perhaps enviable life, his answer surprised me. "There is a little old man, about 80 years old, on Westminster Bridge in London who has been taking pictures there for 65 years. He has a tripod camera, and for a pound he'll take your picture crossing the bridge. He is truly one of the most memorable characters I've met. He laughs a lot and has no teeth. He's learned that it's possible to really enjoy life and be content without a lot of money. He's got enough money to go to the pub in the evening, have a drink with his mates, and laugh. That man is really happy."

I asked Dr. Deepak Chopra what he believes to be the greatest cause of unhappiness. "People are *looking* for happiness, and they're looking for it outside of themselves," he said. "Happiness is our essential state. We don't have to *do* anything to be happy. Just be. It comes from doing nothing—but finding yourself. Happiness

I laugh and try to be playful and silly every day.

Nigel, salesperson

is to be in a certain state of awareness. To have true happiness, you have to be happy for no reason whatsoever. As long as you have a reason for being happy there is a problem, because the reason can be taken away from you. When you are happy for no reason at all, then you are in total bliss and nobody can take that away from you." Roger Gabriel, director of education at the Chopra Center for Wellbeing, added, "If we tie our happiness to an external object like our relationships or our job, then there is always a fear of losing them."

Joy and happiness are part of our being, just like breathing. No one has to remind us to breathe; joy should be that automatic as well. "Yes, but first you have to be alive—really conscious of everything around you," commented my boyfriend, Bernie. "A person can be alive, but dead in spirit, dead in consciousness. That person is not living; they are just going through the motions."

"Joy is not contingent on anything," says psychotherapist Anne Parker, music therapist and facilitator of the Where's the Joy? program at the Life Enhancement Center at Canyon Ranch. Clients come to the centre with a goal: They have a health issue (smoking, weight, stress) they want to change. Anne developed the Where's the Joy? program because she realized that you can talk to people and give them loads of written information, but unless there is some emotional connection, change won't happen. "We put conditions on joy," she explained. "Joy is most connected with process, as opposed to outcome. If we really allow ourselves to be in the process, that is where the joy is. We have become so outcome-oriented in our society, we evaluate everything, including ourselves, by what is produced or accomplished."

Anne asks her achievement-focused clients a question that we should all ask ourselves: *What do you do on a regular basis so that the outcome doesn't matter?* Typically a client may answer, "I play golf." Anne will shoot back, "Well, do you play golf without keeping score?"

So how does she help people connect with themselves? Here's

In the morning, when the sun streams through my window, I stand naked in the warmth of the band of sunlight on the carpet and stretch.
                                        Rose, production manager

where Anne, the music therapist, steps in. "I encourage clients to improvise as they play rhythmic instruments and beat on drums. We put them through a series of playful exercises that are designed to get people out of their heads. They are encouraged not to think in a logical, linear way. This forces them to be in the moment. They laugh a lot. We play games with egg shakers and sing silly songs with nonsense words." After about 40 minutes, Anne asks them to check in with themselves. Comments such as "I haven't laughed like this in years," "I've forgotten what it feels like to have fun," and "I feel free, lighter" are common. Other emotions percolate through as well. "Often people who have cut themselves off emotionally from joy are also cut off from other emotions, so when you begin to open up, sadness, anger, and grief often surface as well."

Here are Anne Parker's suggestions to access the joy within you:

1. Acknowledge those moments when joy is there, because it always is. All it takes is to notice the beauty and wonder in a moment.

2. Instead of a posed picture, keep a photo on your desk of you laughing or being silly.

3. Drive a different route to work and notice the people and scenery.

4. Keep windup toys in your desk drawer. When a meeting gets too serious, unleash your toys and watch the energy change as people are brought into the moment.

5. Set up a humour board at work or at home. Fill it with cartoons, stickers, and buttons. Use a magnetic poetry kit to create words of wisdom you can change on a whim.

6. Keep a jar of soap bubbles handy to blow any time or any place.

7. Sing out loud, alone or with others. While listening to music, play along with whatever is handy—pens, pots, kazoos.

I feel good humming silly little tunes to myself.
Monique, administrative assistant

8. Play with children, climb a jungle gym, go barefoot, dance to music.
9. Be conscious of nature, listen to birds, enjoy the touch and smell of fresh flowers.
10. Put something on your daily to-do list that brings you joy and has no outcome.

After our interview, Anne gave me a gift: a purple bumper sticker that reads "Don't Postpone Joy." I am staring at it as I write this; I decided to place the sign prominently on my desk— beside the clock. We all need reminding, including me. We postpone joy when we inhabit the future—and wait for something big to make us happy. We postpone joy when we inhabit the past—and fester in regret and resentment. We postpone joy when we inhabit the world of end results, expectations, and accomplishments. Joy is found in the present, in the process, in the aliveness of every day, in the hundreds of tiny, ordinary moments we all experience. This is what makes life meaningful and worthwhile. The good dishes are everywhere—in our happy memories, in rituals, in compassionate acts, and in our accepting what is. They're in our courageous spirit, in our meaningful friendships, and in our playfulness. The good dishes are present in simplicity and in silence. Finding an "I love you" scribbled on a Post-it note, cherishing an old chipped bowl because your mom gave it to you before she died, saying a prayer for someone you love, crying once again at the same spot in that old movie, laughing over something silly you and your brother did in high school, pushing a child on a swing—and remembering when it was you, attempting to reach the top of a mountain, noticing a pink-streaked sky, consoling a friend, sticking family photos on your fridge door, enjoying the silence in the forest, inhaling the familiar smell of autumn leaves—the good dishes live in all of these joyful moments.

Where is the joy? Joy is in what moves you deeply, what stirs your soul, what makes your eyes moist, what ignites your heart. Joy

I sing lullabies to my kids at bedtime.

Candice, trade commissioner

is in whatever plucks the strings of passion in your heart, in the very depths of your being. Joy is in the wonder of a child, in the poignancy of life, in the overflowing love for someone. Joy is found in the cycle of life—melting snow making way for the tender green shoots of spring. Joy is in gratitude, in the surprise and privilege of waking up in the morning. Joy is in the temporary, in the moments that don't last, in the day that is gone before we know it, in the life that is gone before we know it.

As you continue on your journey through life, may you live with the knowledge that each day is a gift—a day for you to cherish. Suck the juices out of life! Live like an exclamation mark *feels*! Set your table of life with one full day's worth of meaning for you—a thousand moments to learn, play, laugh, love, give, or just be. When you live and breathe those moments each day, your dishes will be overflowing with joy!

I love when my husband compliments my cooking.

Maggie, teller

INDEX